Moroccan Cookbook

*Traditional Moroccan Recipes
Made Easy*

www.grizzlypublishing.com

Table of Contents

Introduction

First and foremost, I want to give you a massive thank you for purchasing my book, '*Moroccan Cookbook: Traditional Moroccan Recipes Made Easy.*'

Morocco is a little-known country situated on the northern coast of Africa, just a short ferry away from the historically rich European country known as Portugal.

While this country is rarely explored by people from the western world in modern day, Morocco is a place that has truly fascinated travelers for a millennium. It has (and still does, I should add) maintained a unique combination of raw nature and unbelievable architecture that is the envy of the rest of the world.

With the labyrinths of its imperial cities sitting in stark contrast to the dramatic gorges and snowcapped mountain ranges that surround them, it truly is a sight to behold.

In conjunction with these incredible landscapes, we cannot forget the Morocco is also one of the most culturally rich countries in the entire world. With an explicitly unique history, and a vast depth of migration and culture, this amazing country has developed into a place revered by people across the globe.

When you then combine this with exceptionally friendly people, glorious traditions, and a truly joyous way of life, then you have a recipe for success.

Oh, and I should also note that the cuisine is *unbelievable.*

Like many countries on this amazing planet that we call home, the Moroccan diet has been heavily influenced by its neighboring countries. With Europe just a ferry trip away, Mediterranean trade routes maintained for centuries, and the bulk of the African continent just south of the border, Moroccan cuisine has evolved into one of the most diversified in existence.

This evolution has resulted in several important spices playing an integral part of traditional Moroccan cooking, with ingredients such as saffron, mint, olive, oranges, and lemons, frequently appearing in a variety of dishes.

And when you combine these with Moroccan favorites chicken, lamb, beef, and their most well-known grain, couscous? Well, it's pretty damn apparent that you have a recipe (pun intended, of course) for success.

While the food is of course amazing, it would be negligent of me to fail to mention the importance that this cuisine holds in Moroccan culture. You see, over time, the local food and its preparation has slowly become so much more than just 'cooking'.

It has become a very personal way of expressing Moroccon history and the collective identity of its population.

It offers a way to bring family and friends together over a single – and delicious – common interest.

It is a way of life.

So, with all of this in mind, I would have to say that Moroccan cuisine is among the most varied (and dare I say, best) in the world. It not only reflects an amazing collaboration between history and culture, but also provides insight into the lovely people that inhabit this great country.

So, sharpen your knives, prepare your ingredients, and light up the stovetop, because your about to take a trip to Morocco!

Ras El Hanout (Moroccan Spice Mix)

Yield: 8 tablespoons

Ingredients:

- 2 teaspoons ground nutmeg
- 2 teaspoons ground coriander
- 2 teaspoons ground cumin
- 2 teaspoons ground ginger
- 2 teaspoons turmeric
- 2 teaspoons salt
- 2 teaspoons cinnamon
- 1 ½ teaspoons sugar
- 1 ½ teaspoons paprika
- 1 ½ teaspoons ground black pepper
- 1 teaspoon cayenne pepper
- 1 teaspoon cardamom powder
- 1 teaspoon ground allspice
- ½ teaspoon ground cloves

Method:

1. Combine spices and mix thoroughly.
2. Store in an airtight container.

Harissa (Chili Paste Condiment)

Yield: 1 cup sauce (5 portions)

Ingredients:

- 3 or 4 large cloves of garlic
- 2 large handfuls (approx. 3.5 ounces) dried red chili peppers
- 1 to 2 tablespoons lemon juice
- 1 teaspoon salt
- dash of olive oil
- ½ teaspoon cumin seeds (optional)
- ½ teaspoon ground coriander seeds (optional)
- ½ teaspoon ground caraway seeds (optional)

Method:

1. Start by removing the stems and seeds from the dried chili peppers and place them in a bowl.
2. Bring four cups of water to a boil and pour it over the chili peppers; leave the peppers to soften for 30 minutes to an hour.
3. While the peppers are soaking, heat a skillet over medium heat until hot.
4. Add the whole spices and toast until fragrant, stirring constantly, for about a minute.
5. Remove the pan from the heat and grind the spices with a mortar and pestle or spice grinder. Set aside.
6. Drain the chili peppers and gently squeeze out excess water with a paper towel.

7. Using a mortar and pestle (or a blender or mini food processor) grind the chili peppers, garlic, salt and spices to a paste.

8. Add the lemon juice and just enough olive oil to moisten the harissa to desired consistency. Taste and adjust seasoning.

9. Store unused harissa in an airtight glass container in the fridge. For long storage, lightly top the harissa with a little oil before closing.

Chapter One: Moroccan Breakfast Recipes

Khobz (Moroccan Bread)

Yield: 2 loaves

Ingredients:

- 4 cups flour (high-gluten or bread flour preferred)
- 2 teaspoons salt
- 2 teaspoons sugar
- 2 tablespoons vegetable oil
- 1 ¼ cups warm water
- 1 tablespoon yeast (active dry)

Method:

10. First, prepare two baking sheets by lightly oiling them or by dusting the pans with a little cornmeal or semolina.
11. Mix the flour, salt, and sugar in a large bowl. Make a large well in the center of the flour mixture and add the yeast.
12. Add the oil and the water to the well, stirring with your fingers to dissolve the yeast first, and then stirring the entire contents of the bowl to incorporate the water into the flour.
13. Turn the dough out onto a floured surface and begin kneading the dough, or use a stand mixer fitted with a dough hook. If necessary, add flour or water in very small amounts to make the dough soft and pliable, but not sticky. Continue kneading for 10 minutes by hand

(or 5 minutes by machine), or until the dough is very smooth and elastic.

14. Divide the dough in half and shape each portion into a smooth circular mound. (If you prefer, you can divide the dough into four to six smaller loaves instead.) Place the dough onto the prepared pans, cover with a towel and allow it to rest for 10 to 15 minutes.

15. After the dough has rested, use the palm of your hand to flatten the dough into circles about ¼-inch thick. Cover with a towel and let rise about 1 hour (longer in a cold room), or until the dough springs back when pressed lightly with a finger.

16. Heat an oven to 435 F/225 C.

17. Create steam vents by scoring the top of the bread with a very sharp knife or by poking the dough with a fork in several places. Bake the bread for about 20 minutes—rotating the pans about halfway through the baking pans—or until the loaves are nicely colored and sound hollow when tapped. Transfer the bread to a rack or towel-lined basket to cool.

Harcha (Moroccan Semolina Pan-Fried Flatbread)

Serves: 6-8

Ingredients:

- 3 tablespoons sugar
- 2 cups (350 grams) fine semolina (not durum flour)
- 2 teaspoons baking powder
- ½ to ¾ cup (120 to 180 milliliters) milk
- ½ cup (125 grams) soft or melted butter
- ¼ teaspoon salt
- ¼ cup coarse semolina (optional)

Method:

1. First, blend together the fine semolina, sugar, baking powder, and salt in a mixing bowl. Add the butter, and blend with your hands or a wooden spoon just until the mixture is the consistency of sand and the semolina grains have all been moistened.
2. Add ½ cup milk and mix until dough forms. It should be quite moist, wet almost, and easily packed into a large mound. Add additional milk if necessary, to achieve this consistency.
3. Shape the dough into balls any size that you like and leave the dough to rest a few minutes.
4. Preheat a griddle or frying pan over medium-low heat. While the griddle is heating, roll the balls in the coarse semolina (if using) and flatten each ball into a disc about ¼-inch thick, or a bit thicker if you like.

5. Cook the harcha over fairly low heat, about 5 to 10 minutes on each side, until they turn a pale to medium golden color. Flip only once, and check occasionally to be sure the harcha aren't coloring too quickly, as they need some time to cook all the way through.
6. Serve immediately with jam, cheese, or butter.

Notes:

- Coating the cakes in coarse semolina before frying is optional but creates a nice appearance and texture.
- Harcha stores well in the freezer. Reheat them in a pan or in a 350 F (180 C) oven for a few minutes.
- Dip the harcha in syrup made from melted butter and honey. To make the syrup, heat equal portions of the butter and honey until bubbly and hot.

Krachel (Moroccan Sweet Rolls with Anise and Sesame)

Servings: 12-15

Ingredients:

- 4 ½ cups flour
- 2 teaspoons anise seeds
- 2 medium-large eggs (lightly beaten)
- 2 tablespoons orange flower water
- 1 tablespoon yeast
- 1 ½ teaspoons salt
- ¾ cup warm milk
- ½ cup sugar
- ½ cup butter (melted or very soft)
- egg wash made from 1 egg beaten with 1 tablespoon milk
- 1 tablespoon golden sesame seeds (for sprinkling on the rolls)

Method:

1. Start by dissolving the yeast in a few tablespoons of warm water and set aside.
2. Combine the flour, sugar, salt and anise seeds in a large mixing bowl. Add the eggs, the butter, the oil, the orange flower water, the yeast, and the milk. Mix to form a very soft, sticky dough.
3. If you find the dough is too sticky to handle, add the smallest amount of flour necessary to be able to knead the dough. If the dough lacks stickiness, work in additional warm milk or water a few tablespoons at a time.

4. Knead the dough on a lightly floured surface (or in a stand mixer with a dough hook) for about 10 minutes, or until very smooth. (For the desirable light-textured rolls, it's necessary to have the dough somewhat sticky; you'll find that it becomes much easier to handle after its first rising.)

5. Transfer the dough to an oiled bowl and turn the dough over once to coat it with oil. Cover the bowl with a towel and leave the dough to rise until doubled – Usually, this takes about one to one-and-a-half hours, but leave the dough to rise longer if necessary.

6. After the dough has risen, punch it down, gather it up and turn it over. Cover with the towel and leave for a second rising for about an hour (longer in cool weather), until light and spongy.

7. Turn the dough out onto your work surface and divide it into 12 to 15 smooth, evenly shaped balls. Place the balls of dough two inches apart on an oiled baking sheet (or a pan lined with parchment paper).

8. Allow the dough to rest a few minutes, then flatten the balls of dough. Cover the baking sheet with a towel and leave the dough to rise another hour or longer, or until the rolls are very light and puffy.

9. Preheat an oven to 450 F (230 C). Brush the tops and sides of the rolls with the egg wash and sprinkle the rolls with sesame seeds.

10. Bake the krachel for 15 to 20 minutes, or until rich golden brown. Transfer the rolls to a rack to cool.

Notes:

- Be sure that the milk is warm to the touch but not hot. Hot liquids will kill yeast, while cool liquids will not activate it.

- Be patient with the rising time; the dough is quite rich and may take a while to rise properly.
- Rotating the tray from front to back halfway through baking will help ensure even browning.
- If the rolls aren't well-browned after 20 minutes of baking, place them under a broiler for a minute. Watch the rolls carefully, or they'll burn!
- Krachel store well in plastic storage bags in the freezer. They can be warmed in the microwave directly from the freezer without drying out. The trick is to avoid making the rolls too hot.
- If reheating krachel in an oven, enclose the rolls in foil to keep them from becoming hard and dry.
- Remember to allow for ample rising time, particularly in cooler weather.

Variations:

- To make a lighter, less-rich sweet dough for the krachel, reduce the butter to 4 or 5 tablespoons. You can also reduce the sugar slightly and use only 1 egg. Adjust the amount of liquid as necessary to form a soft, slightly sticky dough.
- Although not traditional, using Crisco shortening in place of the butter will yield a very light, fluffy roll.

Khlea and Egg

Serves: 2-4

Ingredients:

- 4 heaped tablespoons khlea
- 6 medium-large eggs
- pinch of salt
- pinch of cumin
- freshly ground black pepper
- a very small amount of fresh parsley (finely chopped)
- 1 tablespoon double (heavy) cream (optional)

Method:

1. Beat the eggs lightly with a fork, with the pinch of salt.
2. Heat the tagine on medium high heat over a diffuser.
3. Add your cold khlea to the cool tagine and wait for the tagine to heat up and the fat to melt. This might take up to 10 minutes. Give it a stir every now and then.
4. When the fat has melted, scoop some out, I usually get rid of about 1 - 2 tablespoons, depending on how much fat was clinging to the meat. Do not add the fat back to your cold khlea in the jar. If you like, you can use it in another dish but in the interest of food safety, do it within the next couple of hours.
5. Stir the khlea a little and let it warm up for about 30 seconds.
6. Pour the beaten egg into the tagine. Now it's not going to sizzle up like it would if you're using a frying pan.
7. Let it settle for about 20 - 30 seconds, then stir it, breaking it up, like you would, when making scrambled

eggs. Continue doing this for about 5 minutes, let it set, stir, set and stir. You'll only need to do this about 3 - 4 times.

8. When the eggs look like they are losing most of their liquid, drizzle in the cream, if using. Stir once again if the egg isn't too set. If you can't stir, just leave the cream to be absorbed.

9. When the egg tagine looks like it's almost cooked, take it off the heat, sprinkle the cumin, pepper and chopped parsley all over and serve immediately, with any type of bread you fancy.

Notes:

- Making this in a frying pan, will drastically cut down the cooking time, to about 5 minutes.

Shakshouka (Moroccan Eggs Tagine)

Yield: 2-3

Ingredients:

- 4-6 free-range eggs
- 3 tablespoons olive oil
- 2-3 button mushrooms (sliced)
- 2 rashers of bacon (diced into cubes)
- 1 ½ cups diced tomatoes (tinned or fresh)
- 1 red or brown onion (roughly diced)
- 1 medium red pepper (capsicum/bell pepper), sliced or diced
- 1 garlic clove (chopped)
- ½ long red chili (finely diced)
- ½ teaspoon salt
- ½ teaspoon ground cumin
- ½ teaspoon paprika
- ½ teaspoon ground coriander seed powder
- ½ dried or fresh oregano leaves (parsley or thyme can be used instead)
- ½ teaspoon turmeric powder (optional) – alternatively, use 1+ 1/2 teaspoons of pre-mixed moroccan spice mix
- fresh parsley and/or coriander (cilantro), roughly chopped

Method:

1. First, heat a teaspoon of olive oil over medium-high heat in a deep-frying pan and add the bacon. Cook until crispy, then remove to a bowl but reserve the fat in the frying pan.

2. Add the remaining olive oil. Add the onions, chili and peppers and sauté for 3-4 minutes, until slightly softened. Season with salt and add the mushrooms and garlic. Cook for a minute, stirring.

3. Then add back the bacon and spices, stir for 30 seconds allowing the aromas to be released. Add the tomatoes, stir and cover with the lid. Cook on medium-low heat for 10-12 minutes, giving it a stir a few times.

4. Using a spoon, make small wells in the tomato mix and crack an egg into each, letting the egg whites to spill over the edges. Sprinkle each egg yolk with a little salt and pepper, cover with a lid and cook on medium-low heat until the egg whites settle and firm up but the egg yolks remain gooey, about 5 minutes. It's very easy to overcook the eggs this way, so it's best to leave them slightly under-cooked as they will keep cooking while getting served.

5. Serve the eggs in the cooking dish sprinkled with some fresh parsley and coriander.

Notes:

- Use a heat proof tagine to cook the tomato base and the eggs but you can use a cast iron or other deep-frying pan or a saucepan with a lid. You can cook this dish on the stove top but you can also bake it in the oven once the eggs have been added to the sauce. I would recommend 15 minutes at 175 C/345 F.

Moroccan Omelet

Serves: 1

Ingredients:

- 8 grape tomatoes (halved, or quartered if large)
- 1 teaspoon fresh lemon juice
- 1 small clove garlic (minced)
- 1 medium-large egg plus 3 large egg whites (beaten)
- ¾ cup baby spinach
- ½ cup canned chickpeas (rinsed and drained)
- ¼ small red onion, diced (about ¼ cup)
- ¼ cup low-sodium vegetable broth
- ¼ avocado (sliced)
- 1/8 teaspoon ground cumin
- pinch each ground coriander, turmeric, cinnamon and black pepper

Method:

1. Cook onion in broth in a nonstick skillet over low heat until translucent, about 6 minutes.
2. Add tomatoes, lemon juice, garlic, spices and chickpeas; cook, stir-ring occasionally, until tomatoes have cooked down slightly, 3 to 4 minutes. Transfer to a bowl.
3. Wipe skillet and mist with olive oil spray. Pour in eggs, then spinach; cook until eggs set, 4 minutes.
4. Fold omelet; plate, top with chickpea mix and garnish with avocado.

Moroccan Sausage and Egg Tagine

Serves: 4

Ingredients:

- 8 oz./225 g. merguez (or other sausage)
- 6 medium-large eggs
- 2 medium tomatoes (peeled, seeded and chopped)
- 1 medium-large onion (finely chopped)
- ½ teaspoon salt
- ½ teaspoon cumin
- ¼ teaspoon black pepper (or 1/8 teaspoon cayenne pepper)
- handful of olives (green pitted, sliced)
- small handful of chopped cilantros (or parsley)
- salt to taste
- cumin to taste
- chopped cilantro (or parsley), garnish

Method:

1. First, gather the ingredients.
2. Cook the sausage in a large skillet or in the base of a tagine until the meat tests done. If there is a large amount of fat from the sausage, remove the excess, leaving enough to continue cooking. If the sausage was low-fat, you may need to add a little olive oil to the pan at this point.
3. Add the onion, tomatoes, olives and seasoning and cook for about 5 minutes. Pour the eggs directly over the sausage and veggies. Break the yolks, and allow the eggs to simmer until set.

4. To help this along, you can lift the edges of the eggs as they cook and tip the pan to allow uncooked egg to run underneath and cook faster. If cooking the eggs in a tagine, cover the eggs and allow them to poach until done.
5. Dust the top of the cooked eggs with cumin and salt to taste, garnish with a little chopped parsley, and serve.

Baghrir (Moroccan Pancakes)

Servings: 8

Ingredients:

- 2 ½ cups warm water
- 1 cup farina flour
- ½ tablespoon dry yeast
- ½ cup all-purpose flour
- ½ tablespoon baking powder
- a dash of salt, about 1/8th teaspoon

Method:

1. Start by combining water, yeast, flour, semolina and salt in your blender, pulse until everything mixes well together.
2. Add the Baking powder and mix again.
3. Place in a container and cover to rise, will take approximately 30 minutes.
4. After 30 minutes, the batter should be thin and not thick as the usual pancakes. *
5. Heat an 8" skillet over medium heat, pour about 1/2 cup of the batter into the skillet. Batter should spread to the edges of the skillet, if not then thin it with more water. see notes for clarification.
6. Small holes should appear all over the surface, continue cooking until no obvious uncooked surface appears. Took me 2 minutes to be completely cooked. **
7. Let them cool down a bit before serving.
8. Serving suggestions: Traditionally, these are enjoyed with butter and honey. Also, for a savory twist,

sometimes can be rolled over olive oil and hard-boiled eggs (cut into small pieces. Practically, this can be enjoyed with your favorite syrup.

Notes:

- *If the batter is not thin, add water in terms of 1 Tablespoons until it gets to the right consistency.
- ** If the pancakes start to curl up at the edges, you know it is overcooked.

Msemen (Square Laminated Pancakes)

Servings: 20

Ingredients:

- 3 ½ cups white flour, all purpose or bread
- 2 teaspoon sugar
- 2 teaspoon salt
- 1 ½ cups warm water (not hot)
- ½ cup fine semolina or durum flour
- ¼ teaspoon dry yeast (less in very warm weather)

For folding the msemen:

- 1 cup vegetable oil (more if needed)
- ½ cup fine semolina (can use coarser caliber if you like)
- ¼ cup very soft unsalted butter (more if needed)

Method:

Make the msemen dough:

1. First, mix the dry ingredients in a large bowl. Add the water and combine to make a dough.
2. Knead the dough by hand (or with a mixer and dough hook) until very smooth, soft and elastic but not sticky. Adjust water or flour as necessary to achieve that texture.
3. Divide the dough into balls the size of small plums. Be sure the top and sides of the balls are smooth. Transfer the balls of dough on an oiled tray, cover loosely with plastic and leave to rest for 10 to 15 minutes.

4. While the dough is resting, set up a work area. You'll need a large flat surface for spreading and folding the dough. Set out bowls of vegetable oil, semolina and very soft butter.
5. Set your griddle or large frying pan on the stove, ready to heat up.

Shape the msemen:

1. Generously oil your work surface and your hands. Dip a ball of dough in the oil and place it in the center of your work space.
2. Using a light touch and quick sweeping motion from the center outward, gently spread the dough into a paper-thin, roughly shaped circle. Oil your hands as often as needed so that they slide easily over the dough.
3. Dot the flattened dough with butter and sprinkle with semolina. Fold the dough into thirds like a letter to form an elongated rectangle. Dot again with butter, sprinkle with semolina, and fold again into thirds to form a square.
4. Transfer the folded dough to the oiled tray and repeat with the remaining balls of dough. Keep track of the order in which you folded the squares.

Cooking the msemen:

1. Heat your griddle or frying pan over medium heat until quite hot. Starting with the first msemen you folded, take a square of dough and place on your oiled work surface. Oil your hands and pat the dough firmly to flatten it to double its original size.

2. Transfer the flattened square to the hot griddle and cook, turning several times, until cooked through, crispy on the exterior and golden in color. Transfer to a rack.

3. Repeat with the remaining squares, working with them in the order in which they were folded. You can flatten and cook several at a time if your pan or griddle can accommodate them.

4. When each msemen has cooled for a minute or two, pick it up from opposite ends and gently flex it for a few seconds with a quick back and forth, see-saw motion. This helps separate the laminated layers from each other.

5. Serve the msemen immediately, or allow to cool completely before freezing.

Reheating and serving msemen:

1. Msemen can be reheated directly from the freezer in a frying pan placed over medium-low heat, or directly on the rack in a preheated 350° F (180° C) oven.

2. To make the traditional Moroccan syrup for dipping, heat equal portions of unsalted butter and honey in a frying pan. When hot and just beginning to bubble, turn off the heat. Dip the warm msemen into the syrup to coat the pancake on both sides.

Notes:

- You can make msemen as small or as large as you like. I prefer to keep them small as described here.

- If you don't have a double griddle, use two or three frying pans on different burners for more efficient cooking.
- Instead of all vegetable oil, you can use a mix of oil and melted butter.
- Some of the white flour can be replaced by whole wheat flour. Adds nice flavor, but the final product might not be as crispy.
- You can also use a mix of half white flour and half semolina. It yields msemen with coarser texture. It's my preferred mix when making meloui, a round, coiled cousin of msemen.

Mlaouis

Serves: 8-10

Ingredients:

Main dough:

- 350 g of strong white bread flour
- 260-290 ml of water (lukewarm)
- 150 g of fine semolina flour
- 1 ½ teaspoon of salt
- ½ teaspoon of dried instant yeast (1 ½ teaspoon for mlaoui mkhamrine)

For shaping and laminating:

- 200 g of fine semolina flour
- 100 g of butter (at room temperature with a cream-like texture)
- 100 ml of vegetable oil

Method:

Prepare the dough:

1. First, mix the yeast with a few tablespoons of barely warm water in a small glass. Stir.
2. Place the flours, salt and yeast in a bowl (each in one side). Add the water to ¾ and start mixing either by hand or by machine.
3. The dough needs to be thoroughly kneaded to become smooth and soft without being sticky. It takes about 20 minutes by hands and 10 minutes with a KitchenAid.

4. The achieve the desired dough texture, gradually add the other ¼ of water according to the absorption of the flours used.

5. You could leave the dough, covered, to rest for 15 min (in cold weather) or skip this step if the weather is too warm. For Mlaouis Mkhamrine, let the dough rise for 45-60 min at room temperature.

Shape Mlaouis the easy method:

1. Oil your hands as well as the dough. Depending how big or small you want the Mlaouis to be. Form slightly thick sausages and roll them. Their length will define the width of Mlaouis. At all times, you should keep the dough as well as the hands oiled.

2. Place each dough sausage on a generously oiled surface. We usually use a big tray where we place them all. Roll the dough balls in oil and cover with foil or a plastic. Set aside to rest for 10 min. Usually, by the time you're done with the whole dough, you could go back to the first one you shaped and start shaping a Meloui.

3. Oil the worktop, try to flatten the dough and stretch it in length at the same time. In this method, your dough does not have to be thin to a see-through condition.

4. You could also start the Meloui shaping the same way we start Msemmen shaping by folding the outer two thirds of a see-through layer of dough on the middle third.

5. Smear with butter and sprinkle with fine semolina flour. Avoid tearing the dough.

6. Now, hold one end of dough with one hand and roll it from the other end with the other while stretching. Keep rolling tight while leaving the edges neat. It should look like this (see pictures below).

7. Tuck the ends inside and set aside for 10 min.

Second method for shaping Mlaoui:

1. Literally start the same way we do for Msemmen. Once the two thirds of the thin dough layer are folder on the middle one without getting to the square shape. Smear the dough with butter and sprinkle it with fine semolina flour in length. Fold the dough again (3rd picture top right).
2. Stretch the dough in length again. Again, a tiny bit of butter and a sprinkle of semolina flour.
3. Shaping Mlaouis second method. 2 rolls in the middle of Msemmen waiting to be flattened to round-shaped Mlaouis
4. Like the previous method, hold one end of dough with one hand and roll it from the other end with the other while stretching. Keep rolling tight while leaving the edges neat.

Flatten Mlaoui rolls:

1. Flatten the first roll you made to 2 mm thick round Meloui.
2. Set aside while you carry on with the rest of the dough rolls. This allows them to proof a bit (15-20 min).
3. Pan-fry each one on medium-heat for 3 mins or so.
4. Plain and khlii-filled Mlaouis being pan-fried.
5. Serve warm with a good glass of hot tea.
6. Freeze extra Mlaouis once cooled.

Batbout (Moroccan Pita Bread)

Servings: 20

Ingredients:

- 3 cups white flour (preferably bread flour or high-gluten)
- 3 tablespoons olive oil or vegetable oil
- 2 tablespoons sugar
- 2 cups durum flour or fine semolina
- 2 teaspoons salt
- 2 cups warm water (approx.)
- 1 tablespoon dry yeast
- 1 cup whole wheat flour

Method:

1. Start by mixing the yeast with a teaspoon of the sugar in a little warm water; set aside until foamy.
2. Combine the flours, remaining sugar and salt. Add the oil, water and the yeast mixture.
3. Stir to bring the dough together, then knead by hand on a floured surface, or with a mixer and dough hook, until smooth and supple, but not sticky. Add flour or water in small increments as needed to make a soft, manageable dough.
4. Shape portions of the dough into smooth balls about the size of plums. Arrange the balls on a lightly floured surface with at least an inch between balls. Cover with a towel and leave the dough to rest for 10 to 15 minutes.
5. When the dough has rested, dust your work surface with flour or fine semolina and roll each ball out into a thin round about 1/8" (0.3 cm) thick. Place on a cotton

sheet or towel and cover. Leave to rise for an hour or a little longer, until light and puffy.

6. Heat a large pan or griddle over medium heat for several minutes until very hot. Carefully transfer the batbout in batches to the pan. Gently turn the batbout as soon as set (after about 10 to 15 seconds) before air bubble being to appear on the surface.

7. Continue cooking the batbout, turning gently several more times, until they have puffed with air and are browned on both sides.

8. Transfer the cooked batbout to a rack or towel-lined basket to cool. Store completely cooled batbout in the freezer.

Notes:

- Make sure to fully preheat your griddle or frying pan. I leave my double griddle to heat up for a full five minutes before cooking the batbout. You can slightly lower the heat after you start cooking if you feel the batbout are browning too quickly.
- It's important to handle the batbout gently while transferring to the pan and while cooking. Rough handling can cause cracks which won't allow the batbout to fill with air.
- When turning puffed batbout in the pan, or when transferring cooked batbout to a rack, be careful of burns which can occur when hot steam escapes from a crack.
- On very cold days, you may need to allow more time for the batbout to rise. Conversely, on very hot days or in hot, dry climates, the batbout can not only rise quickly, but develop a dry exterior on the dough that's prone to cracking.

- If you roll batbout on the thick side, they may not puff up when cooked. In that case, you can gently pry or slice them open to create a pocket for fillings.
- Instead of shaping balls, some cooks like to roll out the dough and cut out rounds with a glass or other biscuit cutter. The scraps can get gathered and kneaded together, then covered and left to rest for 10 to 15 minutes to roll out again.
- I reserve a heavy cotton sheet for making batbout; it fully covers my kitchen table and easily folds over the batbout to cover them while they rise.

Sfenj (Moroccan Donuts)

Servings: 14

Ingredients:

- 500 gr plain flour
- 240ml lukewarm water
- 1 teaspoon salt
- 1 tablespoon dry active yeast
- ¼ teaspoon caster sugar to activate the yeast
- vegetable oil (for frying)
- 250 gr icing sugar sifted for the glaze (optional)
- 2 tablespoon milk for the glaze (optional)

Method:

1. First, activate the dry yeast by adding ¼ teaspoon of sugar and a tablespoon of lukewarm water in a small bowl. Stir with a fork and leave for 5 to 10 minutes until foamy.
2. Transfer the flour, the salt and the water in a large bowl and combine all the ingredients. You should obtain a very sticky dough. If the dough is not sticky (almost like a batter consistency but thicker), add a few tablespoons of water until you obtain the right consistency.
3. Flour a worktop and knead the dough for 10 minutes until very elastic. It will be a bit challenging in the beginning as the dough is very sticky but it will get easier after a couple of minutes.
4. Transfer the dough back in the bowl and cover with cling film and let the dough rest for 4 hours in a warm place, until the dough triples in size.

5. When ready to deep fry the donuts, heat up 6 cm (2.5 inches) of frying oil in a deep pan over medium high-heat until it reaches 180 C (350 F).
6. Dip your hands in water (to help handling the dough) and pull off a piece of dough the size of a plum. Make a hole in the center of the dough and stretch it to make a wide ring. Quickly and carefully transfer the ring of dough into the warm frying oil.
7. Fry on both sides turning occasionally, until crisp and golden.
8. Once ready, use a slotted spoon to transfer the donut to a wire rack lined with paper towels.
9. Continue frying the donuts until you've used all the dough. Enjoy very warm with anything yummy such as sugar, honey, or icing sugar glaze.
10. To make the icing sugar glaze, transfer the sifted icing sugar and milk into a medium sized bowl and slowly stir until smooth.

Notes:

- Sfenj are typically enjoyed warm, don't hesitate to reheat them if they've cooled before you serve them.

Classic Harira (Moroccan Tomato, Lentil, and Chickpea Soup)

Servings: 6-8

Ingredients:

- ½ pound meat (lamb, beef or chicken; uncooked, chopped into ½-inch pieces)
- 3 tablespoons vegetable oil
- 3 tablespoons tomato paste (mixed evenly into 1 or 2 cups of water)
- 3 cups water
- 2 to 3 tablespoons dried lentils (picked over and washed)
- several soup bones (optional)

For the stock:

- 6 medium-large tomatoes (about 2 pounds; peeled, seeded and pureed)
- 1 or 2 stalk celery (with leaves; finely chopped)
- 1 ½ teaspoons pepper
- 1 teaspoon ground cinnamon
- 1 tablespoon ground ginger
- 1 tablespoon kosher salt
- 1 bunch cilantro (finely chopped to yield about ¼ cup)
- 1 bunch fresh parsley (finely chopped to yield about ¼ cup)
- 1 large onion (grated)
- 1 handful of dried chickpeas (soaked and then peeled)

34

- ½ teaspoon turmeric (or ¼ teaspoon yellow colorant)
- smen (optional)
- 2 to 3 tablespoons rice (uncooked; or uncooked broken vermicelli, optional)

Method:

Before you begin cooking the soup:

1. First, gather the ingredients.
2. Wash the herbs and drain well.
3. Pick the parsley and cilantro leaves from their stems. Small pieces of stem are all right, but discard long, thick pieces with no leaves.
4. Finely chop them by hand or with a food processor.
5. Soak and skin the chickpeas. (You might want to soak them the night before you cook.)
6. Peel, seed and puree the tomatoes in a blender or food processor. Or, stew the tomatoes and pass them through a food mill to remove the seeds and skin.
7. Pick through the lentils and wash them.
8. Assemble the remaining ingredients and follow the steps below.

Brown the meat:

1. Put the meat, soup bones and oil into a 6-quart or larger pressure cooker.
2. Over medium heat, cook the meat for a few minutes, stirring to brown all sides.
3. Make the Stock
4. Add the cilantro, parsley, celery, onion, chickpeas, smen (if using), spices and tomatoes. Stir in 3 cups of water.

5. Cover tightly, and heat over high heat until pressure is achieved. Reduce the heat to medium, and cook for 20 to 30 minutes. Remove from the heat and release the pressure.

Make the soup:

1. Add the lentils, tomato paste mixture, and 2 quarts of water to the stock.
2. Set aside (but don't add yet) either the rice or vermicelli.
3. Cover the pot and heat the soup over high heat until pressure is achieved. Reduce the heat to medium and continue cooking.
4. **If adding rice:** Cook the soup on pressure for 30 minutes. Release the pressure, and add the rice. Cover, and cook with pressure for an additional 15 minutes.
5. **If adding vermicelli:** Cook the soup on pressure for 45 minutes. Release the pressure, and add the vermicelli. Simmer the soup, uncovered, for 5 to 10 minutes or until the vermicelli is plump and cooked.

Thicken the soup:

1. While the soup is cooking, make a (soup thickener) by mixing together the 1 cup of flour with 2 cups of water. Set the mixture aside, and stir or whisk it occasionally.
2. The flour will eventually blend with the water. If the mixture is not smooth when you're ready to use it, pass it through a sieve to remove lumps.
3. Once the rice (or vermicelli) has cooked, taste the soup for seasoning. Add salt or pepper if desired.
4. Bring the soup to a full simmer. Slowly — and in a thin stream — pour in the flour mixture. Stir constantly and

keep the soup simmering so the flour doesn't stick to the bottom.

5. You will notice the soup beginning to thicken when you've used approximately half the flour mixture. The thickness of harira is up to you. Some like to thicken the broth so that it achieves a cream-like consistency.

6. Simmer the thickened soup, stirring occasionally, for 5 to 10 minutes to cook off the taste of the flour. Remove the soup from the heat and serve with some parsley.

Notes:

- If the meat had a lot of fat, expect to see some foaming as you simmer the thickened soup. Skim off the foam and discard it.

- As harira cools in the pot, it's common for a skin to form. Simply stir to blend the skin back into the soup.

- A small wedge of lemon may be served as a garnish; its juice may be squeezed into the bowl of harira.

- When reheating harira, don't bring it to a boil. Heat over medium heat and stir frequently to avoid lentils sticking to the bottom.

- **Preparation Shortcut:** Chop your cilantro, parsley, and celery together in a food processor or blender. Add the peeled and seeded tomatoes, and blend until well-pureed. Add the onion and process until the onion is reduced to small pieces. Proceed with making the stock.

- **Thickening with Egg:** In place of flour and water, 2 or 3 beaten eggs may be used to thicken harira. (If desired, beat the eggs with 1/4 cup fresh lemon juice.) Add the eggs in a thin stream to the simmering soup, stirring constantly. You will see some cooked strands of eggs in the soup as it thickens.

- **Prep and Freeze:** If you plan to cook harira frequently, it's helpful to prep large amounts of key ingredients in advance. Soak and peel chickpeas and drain well before freezing. Chop an ample supply of parsley, cilantro, and celery; measure the mixed herbs by soup bowlfuls and freeze. Peel, seed, and stew tomatoes; puree and freeze in about 2-pound batches.

Hssoua Belboula (Moroccan Barley Soup with Milk)

Servings: 6

Ingredients:

- 8 ½ cups water
- 5 to 6 oz evaporated milk
- 3 tablespoons olive oil
- 2 teaspoon cumin
- 2 cups whole milk
- 2 tablespoons butter (unsalted)
- 1 ½ cups barley grits (medium caliber)
- 1 tablespoon salt
- pepper to taste

Method:

1. First, pick through the barley to remove any debris. Wash the barley grits several times in a large bowl filled with water, draining each time through a sieve. Wash until the water is no longer cloudy.
2. In a small stock pot mix the barley grits, water, olive oil, salt, pepper and cumin.
3. Bring to a simmer and cook over medium-low heat for 30 to 40 minutes, or until the soup is thick like porridge and the grains are tender.
4. Stir several times during cooking, and be careful that the heat is not too high or the soup can boil over.
5. Stir in the milk and bring to a simmer again for a few minutes. Turn off the heat, and stir in the butter and evaporated milk.

6. Taste and adjust seasoning as desired. If you like, garnish each serving with a little cumin and olive oil or a bit of butter.

Notes:

- Adjust the thickness of the soup to your own preference by increasing or reducing the milk.
- The soup can also be made without evaporated milk. Substitute half of the water with milk, being extra careful not to let the soup boil over. When the barley is cooked, thin the soup by stirring in additional milk. Add the butter, and serve.
- Reheat leftover hssoua belboula gently, adding a little water if necessary, to return the soup to its original consistency.

Bissara (Split Peas and Fava Beans Soup/Dip)

Serves: 4

Ingredients:

1. 400 gr dried split peas or fava beans (or a mix of both), soaked overnight
2. 4 garlic cloves
3. 3 tablespoons olive oil (and more for garnish)
4. 2 teaspoons baking soda
5. 1 teaspoon paprika (and more for garnish)
6. 1 teaspoon ground cumin (and more for garnish)
7. 3 tablespoons fresh onions (chopped, for garnish, if desired)
8. salt to taste

Method:

1. Start by draining the peas and/or fava beans, run them through water and drain them again.
2. Transfer the peas and/or fava beans in a large casserole and cover with 1 liter of water (the peas and/or fava beans should be completely covered with water). Add the garlic cloves (unpeeled) and the baking soda.
3. Bring to a boil, cover with a lid and reduce the heat to low. Leave to simmer gently for 20 minutes.
4. Remove the garlic cloves from the casserole, unpeel and mash them. Transfer the mashed garlic, olive oil, paprika, cumin and salt in the casserole.
5. Cover with a lid and leave to simmer for another 20 minutes to allow the peas and/or fava beans to cook and soften. Stir occasionally. If you notice that at this stage the mixture is too dry, add a few tablespoons of water.
6. Once the peas and/or fava beans mixture is completely cooked and soft, run the mixture through a food processor (or pass the mixture through a sieve) to obtain a smooth result.
7. Serve hot with bread in a shallow dish or a bowl with a generous coating of olive oil, a sprinkle of paprika and cumin and some chopped onions if desired.

Loubia (Moroccan Stewed White Beans)

Servings: 6

Ingredients:

- 1 lb. dry white haricot (navy) or Cannellini beans, soaked overnight then drained
- 5 cloves of garlic (finely chopped or pressed)
- 3 tablespoons fresh parsley (chopped)
- 3 tablespoons fresh cilantro (chopped)
- 3 ripe tomatoes (grated)
- 2 teaspoons ginger
- 1 medium onion (grated)
- 1 tablespoon salt
- 1 tablespoon paprika
- 1 tablespoon cumin
- ½ cup olive oil
- ¼ teaspoon turmeric (optional)
- ¼ teaspoon cayenne pepper or fresh chili peppers, to taste (optional)
- 1 lb. beef or lamb, on the bone; or 1 cup dried meat (optional)

Method:

Optional step if using fresh meat:

1. If preparing the white beans with lamb or beef, start by browning the meat in the olive oil over medium heat. (Dried or preserved meat needs no browning.) Then proceed with one of the cooking methods below.

Pressure cooker method:

1. Place all ingredients in a pressure cooker and stir to combine.
2. Add 2 quarts (about 2 liters) of water and bring the liquids to a boil over high heat.
3. Cover, bring to pressure, then reduce heat to medium. Continue cooking with pressure for 40 minutes, or until the beans are tender.
4. If the beans are still fully submerged in sauce, reduce the liquids by simmering uncovered until the sauce is thick and not watery, but still quite ample.
5. Taste and adjust seasoning, if needed. Serve warm.

Conventional pot method:

1. Mix all ingredients in a large, heavy-bottomed pot. Add 2 quarts of water (about 2 liters) and bring to a rapid simmer.
2. Cover and continue simmering the beans over medium heat for about 1 1/2 hours, or until the beans are cooked to desired tenderness and the sauce is thick and no longer watery.
3. During cooking, stir occasionally and add a little water if the liquids reduce before the beans have fully cooked.
4. Taste and adjust the seasoning. Serve warm.

Notes:

- Turmeric is not a traditional ingredient in Moroccan stewed white beans, but if you like, you can add it for color as well as for the health benefits.
- Serve with a spoon or eat by hand by scooping up beans and sauce with crusty bread.
- Refrigerate leftovers once the beans have cooled completely.

- Reheat leftover beans gently over medium-low to medium heat, adding a little water if necessary.

Chapter Two: Moroccan Lunch Recipes

Moroccan Chicken Tagine

Servings: 4-6

Ingredients:

- 8 bone-in, skin-on chicken thighs (about 4 pounds), trimmed of excess skin and fat *(see note)*
- 5 cloves garlic (minced)
- 2 tablespoons all-purpose flour
- 2 tablespoons honey
- 2 large or 3 medium carrots, peeled and cut crosswise into ½-inch-thick coins
- 2 tablespoons fresh cilantro leaves (chopped)
- 1 ¾ cups chicken broth
- 1 lemon
- 1 teaspoon paprika
- 1 teaspoon ground cumin
- 1 tablespoon olive oil
- 1 large yellow onion (halved and cut into ¼-in-thick slices)
- ½ teaspoon ground ginger
- ½ teaspoon ground coriander
- ½ cup greek cracked green olives, pitted and halved *(see note)*
- ¼ teaspoon cayenne pepper
- ¼ teaspoon ground cinnamon
- salt and ground black pepper

Method:

1. Start by combining the spices in a small bowl and set aside. Zest the lemon. Combine 1 teaspoon of the lemon zest with 1 minced garlic clove; set aside.

2. Season both sides of chicken pieces with 2 teaspoons salt and ½ teaspoon pepper. Heat the oil in a large heavy-bottomed Dutch oven or pan over medium-high heat until beginning to smoke. Brown the chicken pieces skin side down in single layer until deep golden, about 5 minutes; using tongs, flip the chicken pieces over and brown the other side, about 4 minutes more.

3. Transfer the chicken to a large plate; when cool enough to handle, peel off the skin and discard. Pour off and discard all but 1 tablespoon of fat from the pan.

4. Reduce the heat to medium. Add the onion and cook, stirring occasionally, until they have browned at the edges but still retain their shape, 5 to 7 minutes (add a few tablespoons of water now and then if the pan gets too dark). Add the remaining minced garlic and cook, stirring, until fragrant, about 30 seconds. Add the spices and flour and cook, stirring constantly, until fragrant, about 30 seconds.

5. Stir in the broth, honey, remaining lemon zest, and ¼ teaspoon salt, scraping the bottom of the pan with a wooden spoon to loosen any browned bits. Add the chicken (with any accumulated juices) back in, reduce the heat to medium-low, cover and simmer for 10 minutes.

6. Add the carrots, cover, and simmer until the chicken is cooked through and the carrots are tender-crisp, about 10 minutes more.

7. Stir in the olives, reserved lemon zest-garlic mixture, cilantro, and 1 tablespoon of the lemon juice; taste the sauce and adjust seasoning with salt, pepper, and more lemon juice, if desired.

8. Serve with couscous.

Note:

- Don't fret too much over trimming the chicken thighs. The skin gets removed midway through the cooking process and most of the fat will cook off and get drained. Cracked green olives are olives that have been 'cracked' or split open before curing, allowing the brine or marinade to penetrate. You can find them in your supermarket's olive bar, or substitute any green olive that you like.

- **Make-Ahead:** After you have completed the step of cooking the carrots, the dish can be refrigerated for up to 2 days. To serve, gently warm on the stove until the chicken is heated through, then proceed to the step where the olives and remaining ingredients are added.

Moroccan Salmon with Nectarine Couscous

Servings: 4

Ingredients:

- 4 4-oz boneless salmon fillets (skin on)
- 1 oz pine nuts (toasted)
- 2 green onions (chopped)
- 1 teaspoon paprika
- ¾ teaspoon ground cumin
- ½ teaspoon ground ginger
- ¼ teaspoon ground cardamom
- ½ teaspoon fresh ground black pepper
- ½ teaspoon sea salt (divided)
- ½ cup whole-wheat couscous
- ½ yellow bell pepper (diced)
- ½ cup nectarine (diced)
- high-heat cooking oil (such as sunflower, safflower, peanut, or grape seed oil), as needed

Method:

1. First, combine paprika, cumin, ginger, cardamom, black pepper and ¼ teaspoon salt in a small bowl. Sprinkle evenly on all sides of salmon, pressing mixture into flesh to adhere.
2. Heat a grill pan on medium-high and lightly brush with cooking oil. Add salmon, skin side up, and cook for 2 minutes. Turn and cook, skin side down, until salmon is opaque throughout, about 5 more minutes.
3. Meanwhile, in a small saucepan, bring ¾ cup water to boil. Stir in couscous and remove from heat. Cover and

let stand for 5 minutes. Fluff with fork and stir in onions, bell pepper, nuts, nectarine and remaining ¼ teaspoon salt. Divide salmon and couscous mixture among serving plates.

Grilled Moroccan Chicken

Servings: 4

Ingredients:

- 1 ½ to 1 ¾ pounds boneless skinless chicken breasts (or chicken tenderloins)
- 3 garlic cloves (minced)
- 2 teaspoons paprika
- 1 teaspoon salt
- 1 teaspoon sugar
- 1 teaspoon ground cumin
- ½ teaspoon ground coriander
- ¼ teaspoon ground ginger
- ¼ teaspoon ground turmeric
- ¼ teaspoon ground cinnamon
- ¼ cup extra virgin olive oil
- 1/8 teaspoon cayenne pepper

Method:

1. First, place chicken breasts between 2 pieces of wax or parchment paper and, using a meat mallet, pound to an even ½-inch thickness. (Skip this step if substituting chicken tenderloins.)
2. Mix all ingredients except chicken together in a small bowl or measuring cup. Place pounded chicken breasts inside 1-gallon zip-lock bag.
3. Add marinade to the bag, press air out and seal shut. Massage marinade into the breasts until evenly coated. Place the bag in a bowl in the refrigerator (to protect

against leakage), and let the chicken marinate for 5-6 hours.

4. Clean grill and preheat to high. Place chicken breasts on grill, spooning marinade over top. Grill, covered, for 2-3 minutes per side. Do not overcook.

Moroccan Meatball Tagine with Lemon and Olives

Servings: 4

Ingredients:

- 500g lamb (minced)
- 250ml lamb stock
- 100g pitted black kalamata olive
- 3 onions (peeled)
- 2 tablespoons olive oil
- 1 teaspoon ground cumin
- 1 teaspoon ground cinnamon
- 1 red chili (deseeded and finely chopped)
- 1 tablespoon tomato purée
- zest and juice 1 unwaxed lemon (quartered)
- pinch cayenne pepper
- small bunch flat-leaf parsley (chopped)
- small bunch coriander (chopped)
- thumb-sized piece ginger (peeled and grated)
- pinch saffron strands
- couscous or fresh crusty bread (to serve)

Method:

1. First, put the onions in a food processor and blitz until finely chopped.
2. Put the lamb, lemon zest, spices, parsley and half the onions in a large bowl, and season.
3. Using your hands, mix until well combined, then shape into walnut-sized balls.

4. Heat the oil in a large flameproof dish, or tagine with a lid, then add the remaining onions, ginger, chili and saffron. Cook for 5 mins until the onion is softened and starting to color.
5. Add the lemon juice, stock, tomato purée and olives, then bring to the boil.
6. Add the meatballs, one at a time, then reduce the heat, cover with the lid and cook for 20 mins, turning the meatballs a couple of times.
7. Remove lid, then add the coriander and lemon wedges, tucking them in between the meatballs.
8. Cook, uncovered, for a further 10 mins until the liquid has reduced and thickened slightly.
9. Serve hot with couscous or fresh crusty bread.

Moroccan Turkey Salad

Servings: 4

Ingredients:

- 500g leftover turkey breast (shredded)
- 250g cherry tomato (halved)
- 100g rocket
- 2 pitta breads
- 2 tablespoons olive oil
- 1 diced aubergine
- 1 tablespoon harissa
- seeds 1 pomegranate or 110g tub pomegranate seeds
- a few mint leaves

Method:

1. Start by tearing the pitta into pieces and fry in the olive oil until crisp. Tip into a bowl, then fry the aubergine for 10 mins until soft.
2. Add to the pitta with the harissa, tomatoes, turkey and rocket. Toss well. Scatter over pomegranate seeds and mint leaves.

Moroccan Kefta Kebab

Servings: 4

Ingredients:

- 1-pound ground beef (or lamb, or a combination of the two)
- 2 teaspoons paprika
- 1 medium onion (chopped very fine or grated)
- 1 teaspoon cumin
- 1 teaspoon salt
- ¼ teaspoon pepper
- ¼ cup fresh parsley (chopped)
- ¼ cup fresh cilantro (chopped)
- 1/8 teaspoon cayenne pepper
- 1 teaspoon cinnamon (optional)
- 3 ounces beef or lamb fat (optional)
- 1 tablespoon chopped mint leaves (excellent with lamb, optional)

Method:

1. First, mix all ingredients together in a large mixing bowl, and let sit for 1 hour or longer to allow the flavors to blend. The kefta is then ready to shape and cook.
2. To make kebabs, take small amounts of kefta and shape them into cylinders or sausage shapes. Skewer the meat, squeezing it to mold it the skewer.
3. Cook over hot coals, approximately 5 minutes each side. (It may take less or more time, depending on how hot the coals are, and how thick you shaped the kefta.)

Watch the kebabs carefully, so you don't dry out the meat.

4. Serve immediately, or wrap in aluminum foil to keep hot while you cook additional kebabs.

Notes:

- If you would like to grind your meat at home, a finer grind is preferred for this dish.
- Traditionally, the meat, fat, spices, and herbs would all be passed through a meat grinder together to blend the flavors better.

Variations:

- You can use lean ground meat, but the classic recipe calls for a higher fat content.
- To vary the recipe, you can add up to a teaspoon each of the following: ground ginger, turmeric, Ras El Hanout or minced garlic.

Moroccan Couscous with Meat and Seven Vegetables

Servings: 6

Ingredients:

For the meat:

- 2 lbs. 3 oz./1 kg. lamb or beef on the bone (cut into large pieces), or 1 whole chicken
- 3 tomatoes (peeled and coarsely chopped)
- 2 teaspoons ginger
- 1 ½ tablespoons salt
- 1 large onion (coarsely chopped)
- 1 tablespoon black pepper
- 1 teaspoon turmeric, or ¼ teaspoon moroccan yellow colorant
- 1 handful of fresh parsley and cilantro sprigs (tied into a bouquet)
- ¼ cup vegetable oil
- about 2 ½ qt./2 ½ l. water
- ¼ cup dry chickpeas, soaked overnight (optional)

For the couscous:

- 2 lbs. 3 oz./1 kg. dry couscous (not instant)
- 2 tablespoons unsalted butter
- 1 tablespoon salt
- ¼ cup/60 ml. vegetable oil
- water

For the vegetables:

- 10 carrots (peeled and halved)
- 3 to 4 turnips (peeled and halved)
- 4 to 5 small zucchinis (ends removed and halved)
- 1 to 2 tomatoes (peeled and quartered)
- 1 to 2 small onions (whole or halved)
- 1 small acorn squash (quartered), or a small section of pumpkin (cut into 3-inch pieces)
- ½ small cabbage (cut into 2 or 3 sections)
- 2 to 3 small sweet potatoes (peeled and halved, optional)
- ½ cup fresh fava beans (optional)
- 1 to 2 jalapeño or chili peppers (optional)

Method:

Make the meat:

1. Start by mixing the meat, onion, tomatoes, oil, and spices in the bottom of a couscoussier.
2. Cook uncovered over medium to medium-high heat, stirring occasionally, for about 15 minutes, or until the meat is browned and the onions and tomatoes have formed a thick sauce.
3. Add the water, the parsley/cilantro bouquet, and the chickpeas, if using. Cover, and bring to a boil over high heat. Reduce the heat to medium, and simmer rapidly for 25 to 30 minutes. (If omitting both meat and chickpeas, simmer for just a few minutes.)

First steaming of couscous:

1. While the meat is cooking, get the couscous ready for its first steaming. Oil the steamer basket and set it aside.
2. Empty the dry couscous into a very large bowl, and work in the vegetable oil with your hands, tossing the couscous and rubbing it between your palms. (This will help prevent the couscous grains from clumping together.)
3. Work in 1 cup of water in the same manner, using your hands to evenly distribute the liquid into the couscous. Transfer the couscous to the oiled steamer basket.
4. Add the cabbage to the meat mixture, and place the steamer basket on top (seal the joint if necessary). Once you see steam rising from the couscous, steam the couscous for 15 minutes.
5. Pour the couscous back into the large bowl and break it apart.
6. When the couscous has cooled enough to handle, gradually work in 2 cups of water and 1 tablespoon of salt with your hands.
7. Again, toss the couscous and rub it between your palms to break up any balls or clumps.
8. Transfer the couscous back into the steamer, taking care not to pack or compress the couscous.

Second steaming of couscous:

1. Add the turnips, carrots, tomatoes, onions, and fava beans (if using) to the pot. Place the steamer basket on top of the couscoussier (seal the joint if necessary), and steam the couscous a second time for 15 minutes,

timing from when you see the steam rising from the couscous.

2. Once the couscous has steamed for 15 to 20 minutes, turn it out into the large bowl again. Break it apart, and let cool a few minutes.

3. If you're serving the couscous with jalapeño peppers, simmer the peppers, covered, in a half-ladle of broth and a little water, for about 40 minutes, or until the jalapeños are tender. (The peppers are typically placed on top of the couscous, and small pieces may be broken off as a condiment.)

Third steaming of couscous:

4. Gradually work 3 cups of water into the couscous with your hands, tossing it and rubbing the grains between your palms. Taste the couscous, and add a little salt if desired.

5. Transfer about half of the couscous to the steamer basket. Again, try to handle the couscous lightly and avoid packing it into the steamer.

6. Add the squash, zucchini, and sweet potatoes, if using, to the couscoussier, and place the steamer basket on top. (Again, seal the joint if necessary.)

7. When you see the steam rise through the couscous, carefully add the remaining couscous to the steamer.

8. Continue cooking, watching for the steam to rise from the couscous. Allow the couscous to steam for a full 15 to 20 minutes. At this point, all of the vegetables should be cooked. Test the vegetables to be sure, cooking longer if necessary.

9. Taste the broth—it should be salty and peppery—and adjust the seasoning if desired.

Serving the couscous and vegetables:

1. Empty the couscous into the large bowl, and break it apart. Mix in the 2 tablespoons of butter with 2 ladles of broth.
2. To serve the couscous, shape it into a mound with a well in the center. Put the meat into the well, and arrange the vegetables on top and all around.
3. Distribute the broth evenly over the couscous and vegetables, reserving one or two bowlfuls to offer on the side for those who prefer more.

Notes:

- If you see steam escaping from between the basket and couscoussier, you'll need to seal the joint. You can do this in several ways: wrap and tie a long piece of damp cloth over the joint, tightly wrap a long piece of kitchen plastic film around the joint, or wrap and drape a long piece of kitchen plastic film onto the rim of the couscoussier, and then place the basket on top.

Loubia (Moroccan Stewed White Beans)

Servings: 4-6

Ingredients:

- 1 pound/500g dry white haricot or cannellini beans (soaked overnight and drained)
- 3 ripe tomatoes (grated)
- 3 cloves of garlic (finely chopped or pressed)
- 2 tablespoons fresh parsley (chopped)
- 2 tablespoons fresh cilantro (chopped)
- 2 teaspoons paprika
- 2 teaspoons cumin
- 1 ½ teaspoons ginger
- 1 medium onion (grated)
- 1 tablespoon salt
- ½ teaspoon cayenne pepper (or to taste, optional)
- ½ cup olive oil

Method:

Pot method:

1. Start by mixing all the ingredients in a large pot.
2. Add 2 quarts/2 liters of water and bring to a simmer.
3. Cover and simmer the beans over medium heat for about 1 ½ hours, or until the beans are tender and the sauce is thick and no longer watery.
4. If the liquids reduce too much during cooking, add a little water to prevent the beans from burning.

5. Adjust the seasoning if desired, and serve. (*Note: that the beans should be quite saucy at serving time. The beans will continue to absorb liquid as they sit, so allow for this if preparing the beans in advance for later serving.*)

Pressure cooker method:

1. Mix all ingredients in a pressure cooker.
2. Add 2 quarts/2 liters of water, and bring to a simmer.
3. Cover, bring to pressure, then cook on pressure over medium heat for about 40 minutes, or until the beans are tender.
4. If the beans are still submerged in sauce, reduce the liquids until the sauce is thickened.
5. Adjust the seasoning if desired, and serve.

Notes:

- White beans can certainly be eaten with a spoon, but they're also very good scooped up like a dip with crusty bread.
- If you want to add lamb or beef, brown the meat (cubed or in 2-inch pieces) in the oil and then proceed with the directions as described.
- Refrigerate leftovers once the beans have cooled completely. If necessary, add a little water when reheating and use no more than medium heat to avoid scorching.

Moroccan Fish with Couscous

Servings: 4

Ingredients:

- 4 firm white fish fillets (6 oz each)
- 2 teaspoon vegetable or olive oil
- 1 ½ tablespoons moroccan seasoning
- 1 tablespoon lemon juice
- 1 teaspoon lemon peel (grated)
- 1 cup couscous
- ½ small red onion (finely chopped)
- ¼ cup slivered almonds (toasted)
- ¼ cup chopped cilantro (plus extra leaves, to serve)
- ¼ cup plain yogurt (to serve)

Method:

1. First, place couscous in a medium heatproof bowl; stir in 1 cup boiling water. Cover with plastic wrap. Let stand for 5 mins or until liquid is absorbed.
2. Using a fork, fluff and separate grains. Stir in nuts, onion, lemon juice, cilantro and 1 teaspoon of the oil.
3. Meanwhile, combine seasoning, lemon peel and remaining 1 teaspoon oil in a small bowl. Rub spice mixture over fish.
4. Heat a large nonstick skillet on medium heat. Add fish to pan; cook for 2-3 mins each side or until browned and cooked through.
5. Spoon couscous onto plates. Top with fish. Serve at once with yogurt and cilantro leaves.

Taktouka (Green Peppers and Tomatoes Moroccan Salad)

Servings: 3-4

Ingredients:

- 4 large tomatoes or 5 medium tomatoes
- 4 tablespoons mixture of fresh parsley and coriander (chopped)
- 3 tablespoons olive oil
- 2 large sweet green peppers such as bell peppers
- 1 teaspoon garlic, about 2 cloves (finely chopped)
- 1 teaspoon paprika
- ½ teaspoon cumin
- ½ teaspoon salt or more to taste
- ½ teaspoon caster sugar
- pinch cayenne pepper

Method:

1. First, preheat your grill or chargrilled pan to high.
2. Place the green peppers on your grill and turn occasionally every 3 to 4 minutes until each side is scorched (lightly burned) and tender.
3. Remove the green peppers from the grill and set aside to cool.
4. Meanwhile, peel, deseed, and roughly chop the tomatoes into 1, 5 cm (1 inch) pieces.
5. Once the green peppers have reached room temperature, peel and deseed and chop them into 1,5 cm (1 inch) pieces.

6. In a large casserole or a deep skillet, heat the olive oil over medium-low heat and add the chopped tomatoes, garlic, spices, herbs, salt and sugar.
7. Cover with a lid for 10 minutes until the tomatoes have softened. Stir occasionally.
8. Uncover, add the chopped green peppers and mix all the ingredients together. Leave to simmer gently for 10 minutes until all the liquids evaporate.
9. Enjoy warm or cold, as a side or a filling in a tasty sandwich.

Moroccan Tuna Bocadillos with Olives, Potatoes and Harissa

Servings: 1-2

Ingredients:

- 1 long french baguette (or baguette roll or khobz)
- 1 15-ounce can of tuna (drained)
- 2 tablespoons olive oil (mayonnaise or vinaigrette, optional)
- 2 tablespoons harissa (or hot sauce)
- 2 hard-boiled eggs (chopped or sliced)
- 1 carrot (diced, boiled or steamed)
- ½ tomato (chopped or sliced)
- ½ potato (diced, boiled or steamed)
- ½ onion (red, minced or slivered, raw)
- ¼ cup olives (sliced, or chopped capers)

- boiled rice
- grated cheese (edam is popular), garnish
- chopped lettuce, garnish

Method:

1. **Prepare any cooked fillers ahead of time:** boil or steam potatoes; boil or steam carrots; boil and chop eggs; boil rice.
2. **Prep your cold ingredients:** slice tomatoes and chop lettuce; chop or sliver an onion; slice olives; grate your cheese.
3. When ready to assemble, arrange all the fillers in one large work area.
4. Slice your baguette or other bread lengthwise. If desired, brush the bread or drizzle it with olive oil or vinaigrette; or, spread it with a little mayonnaise. Add harissa or hot sauce to taste.
5. Stuff the bread with tuna, onion, olives, cooked potatoes and your choice of other ingredients. Typically, the ingredients are used in moderation since a variety of them are being combined.
6. Serve the bocadillos with Moroccan Mint Tea or another beverage.
7. Wrapped well, the sandwiches may be refrigerated for up to two days.

Moroccan Merguez Ragout with Poached Eggs

Servings: 4

Ingredients:

- 1-pound merguez sausage (sliced ½-inch thick)
- 215-ounce cans muir glen fire-roasted tomatoes
- 8 extra-large eggs or 9 large eggs
- 4 large garlic cloves (peeled and minced)
- 2 tablespoons harissa
- 1 large onion (small dice)
- 1 tablespoon ras el hanout
- 1 teaspoon spanish sweet smoked paprika
- 1 teaspoon kosher salt
- ½ cup extra virgin olive oil
- ½ cup roughly chopped cilantro (stems included)
- warm crusty bread (for serving)

Method:

1. First, heat the olive oil in a large frying pan over medium heat. Add the onion and sauté until golden. Toss in the garlic and cook another 2 minutes. Add the merguez and sauté until almost cooked through, about 3 minutes.
2. Lower the heat to medium-low and add the Ras el Hanout, Spanish smoked paprika and salt. Stir to combine and cook for a minute to lightly toast the spices. Add the tomatoes. Turn up the heat to medium and cook until the mixture has thickened slightly, about 5 minutes.

3. Crack the eggs over the mixture, cover and cook until the whites set, but the yolks are still soft.
4. Divide the eggs and ragout among four warm bowls using a large spoon. Top with a sprinkling of cilantro and a teaspoon of Harissa.
5. Serve immediately with crusty bread or Khobz.

Kabda (Moroccan Fried Liver and Onions)

Servings: 2-3

Ingredients:

- 1 lb./500 g fresh calf or lamb liver
- 3 to 4 tablespoons vegetable oil (or olive oil)
- 2 to 3 teaspoons vinegar (or lemon juice)
- 2 or 3 large onions (thinly sliced)
- 1 or 2 tablespoons butter
- 1 tablespoon vegetable oil
- 1 teaspoon cumin
- 1 teaspoon paprika
- 1 teaspoon salt (or to taste)
- ¼ teaspoon black pepper (or to taste)
- 1/8 teaspoon pepper
- pinch of salt
- 1 tablespoon chopped parsley (or cilantro), optional
- ½ teaspoon of sugar (optional)
- 1/8 teaspoon cayenne pepper (optional)
- flour (for dredging the liver, optional)

Method:

1. First, make sure the liver is properly cleaned and trimmed. Slice the liver into thin pieces or steaks and score the edges all around to help prevent the liver from curling while it's frying.
2. Mix the liver with the spices, vinegar, and oil in a bowl and leave to marinate for 30 minutes or longer.

3. In a large skillet, heat the vegetable or olive oil over medium to medium-high heat.
4. Add the sliced onions, a pinch or two of salt and pepper, and stir to coat the onions evenly with the oil.
5. Fry the onions for about 10 minutes, stirring occasionally, until the onions are lightly colored and tender. (Or, you can caramelize the onions. To do this, add ½ teaspoon of sugar and fry the onions over slightly lower heat until well colored and caramelized, about 20 to 30 minutes.)
6. Push the onions to the sides of the pan. If desired, dredge the liver lightly in flour. Add the liver to the pan and fry it for 5 to 7 minutes on each side, or until cooked through.
7. Stir the onions occasionally while the liver is frying.
8. When the liver has cooked, transfer the meat and onions to a plate.
9. Add the tablespoon or two of butter to the pan and swirl the pan to melt the butter and combine it with the juices to form a sauce.
10. Serve the liver and onions immediately with the sauce poured on top. Garnish with a little parsley or cilantro if desired.

Chapter Three: Moroccan Dinner Recipes

Seffa Medfouna (Moroccan Chicken Vermicelli)

Servings: 4-6

Ingredients:

Chicken:

- 2 pounds (1 kg) of chicken drumsticks
- 1-pound (500 grams) onions (grated)
- 2 cinnamon sticks
- 1 tablespoon olive oil
- 1 tablespoon vegetable oil
- 1 teaspoon ground ginger
- ½ teaspoon salt
- ½ teaspoon smen (ghee / clarified butter)
- ¼ cup cilantro (finely chopped)
- ¼ cup parsley (finely chopped)
- ¼ teaspoon black pepper
- ¼ teaspoon ground turmeric
- a pinch of saffron threads
- water to cook the chicken

Dried fruits:

- blanched almonds
- dates, raisins, and walnuts

Vermicelli:

- 1 pound (500 grams) of italian vermicelli (very fine pasta)
- water + salt
- butter

Method:

Making the chicken:

1. Drizzle the olive oil and vegetable oil in a pot. Add the grated onions, chicken spices, cinnamon sticks, and the chicken. Mix all the ingredients together using a wooden spoon.
2. Cover the pot and cook the chicken on medium heat for 5 minutes. Stir the chicken from time to time.
3. After 5 minutes, add the finely chopped parsley and cilantro as well as the smen (ghee). Make sure to adjust the amount of salt you are using in this dish to the saltiness of the ghee you are using. Otherwise, the chicken may become too salty.
4. Mix all the ingredients and add a little bit of water, just enough to cover half the height of the chicken.
5. Cover the pot, increase the heat to medium-high, and let the chicken cook until done.
6. From time to time, check on the chicken, stir it, and add water if necessary. The water should be covering half the height of the chicken until the chicken is cooked.
7. The chicken should be done within 30-40 minutes. Taste the chicken, it should be soft.
8. Remove the chicken from the pot and place it in a bowl.

9. Uncover the pot, increase the heat to high, and let the sauce cook for 10 minutes until the liquids evaporate and the sauce becomes thick and silky.

10. Once the sauce has reduced, turn off the heat, bring back the chicken to the pot, cover and keep it there until ready to serve the dish.

Preparing the dried fruits:

1. You can use any dried fruits of your choice, in the amounts of you want or just skip them.

2. Soak the dates and the raisins in two separate bowls filled with warm water at least 30 minutes before using them.

3. To blanch almonds, just place whole almonds in boiling water for 5 minutes, then rinse them and rub them using a towel. The skin of the almonds will easily be removed.

4. First, we are going to fry the almonds. In a flat pan heat vegetable oil. When the oil is hot, place the blanched almonds in the hot oil and fry until the almonds get a nice golden-brown color.

5. Once done, remove the almonds from oil and place them in a plate covered with paper towel to absorb any excess oil.

6. **Optional:** Take some of the fried almonds and mix, using a food processor, with a bit of orange blossom water and powdered sugar.

7. Steam the raisins and pitted dates separately for 10-15 minutes until they soften up.

Steaming the vermicelli:

1. To steam the vermicelli, you can use a couscous pot. However, feel free to use your regular steamer.
2. Fill the bottom of the couscous pot with water and add ½ lemon.
3. Take 2 tablespoons of the oil where you fried the almonds (or just regular vegetable oil) and using your hand, mix it gently with the vermicelli until it is completely coated with the oil.
4. Place the vermicelli in the top portion of the couscous pot, cover, and steam on medium-high heat until you see the first steam coming out from the vermicelli. This will take around 15-20 minutes.
5. Remove the vermicelli from the top part of the couscous pot, and place in a large plate. Add ½ cup of salted water to the vermicelli, mix with your hands, and let the vermicelli rest for about 5 minutes.
6. Return the vermicelli to the couscous pot and steam again until you see the steam coming out from the vermicelli (this will take around 10 minutes). Note that while the vermicelli was resting, leave the fire on the bottom part of the couscous pot filled with water.
7. Check the vermicelli. If it is not ready, you may have to steam it for a 3rd time.
8. Remove it from the couscous pot, place in a plate, and add a bit of water (not salted this time, if the vermicelli is salty enough).
9. Let it rest for 5 minutes and place back in the couscous pot. Steam for 5-10 minutes until done but make sure not to overcook it, otherwise, it becomes too soft.
10. When the vermicelli is ready, place it in a large plate and fluff it (using forks) with a little bit of butter.

Final steps:

1. In general, prepare the chicken the dried fruits in advance, and the vermicelli just right before serving the dish. Heat the chicken if necessary.
2. To plate the dish first mix the hot vermicelli with the steamed raisins.
3. In a large plate, place a layer of vermicelli. Put the chicken on top of the vermicelli and cover it with the thick sauce.
4. Cover the chicken with the rest of the vermicelli into a dome shape.
5. **Optional:** Place the ground almonds (with powdered sugar and orange blossom water) at the top of the dome.
6. Decorate with the almonds, walnuts, and dates.

Rfissa (Moroccan Chicken with Lentils)

Servings: 6-8

Ingredients:

- 1 (2 -3 lb.) whole chickens

Marinade:

- ½ large onion (grated)
- ½ tablespoon ginger
- ½ tablespoon ras el hanout spice mix
- ½ teaspoon salt
- ½ teaspoon black pepper
- ¼ cup olive oil

Msemmen:

- 5 cups unbleached flour
- 2 teaspoons salt
- 2 teaspoons sugar
- 2 cups water (varies)
- oil

Sauce:

- 5 cups water (divided)
- 2 -3tablespoons smen (can be bought online)
- 1 ½ large onions (cut into strips)
- 1 teaspoon salt
- 1 teaspoon black pepper
- 1 pinch saffron
- 1 bunch parsley (tied together)

- 1 tablespoon fenugreek seeds (not ground)
- 1 cup dry lentils
- ½ tablespoon ginger
- ½ tablespoon ras el hanout spice mix
- ½ teaspoon turmeric
- ¼ cup canola oil

Method:

Chicken:

1. Wash the chicken & marinate it in a mixture of grated onion, olive oil, ginger, ras el hanout, salt, & pepper for at least 2 hours in the refrigerator.

Note: The m'semmen takes the longest to make & it should be started before cooking the chicken. You can make 2 smaller batches instead of 1 large one. One to make before cooking the chicken & the other to make while the chicken is cooking.

M'semmen:

1. In a large bowl mix 2 ½ cups of flour with 1 teaspoon salt and 1 teaspoon sugar. Add enough lukewarm water to the mixture to form a stiff dough. (Flours differ in their ability to absorb moisture so no precise amount can be given. Add a small amount at a time. If you have added too much the mixture will be extra sticky and it will be hard to get off your hands, add a little more flour. The right consistency should allow the dough to pull easily off your fingers).

2. Knead the mixture for 5 minutes until it forms a smooth dough. Pull the dough apart into golf ball size balls, around 12-15.
3. Pour 1 tablespoon of oil onto a large pizza pan. Lightly roll each ball in the oil then place back into the bowl (this helps insure the balls do not dry out).

Note: The next step is where you really should have 2 people. One to form the m'semmen & one to cook it.

1. **Person 1:** Make sure your hands and the pizza pan are well oiled (you will have to keep adding more oil for each ball). Take one ball & gently spread it out with your oiled fingertips stretching the dough in all directions until it is very thin. (It should be thin like paper but you don't want it to pull apart).
2. **Person 2:** Drizzle a small amount of oil in a large frying pan with your fingertips. Heat the pan over medium heat until it gets hot. Lay one sheet of m'semmen in the pan & cook on each side until it has golden spots.
3. Repeat the previous 2 steps until each ball has been cooked. Place the m'semmen on a plate to be used later.
4. In an 8- or 10-quart pressure cooker place 4 cups of water, onion strips, parsley, spices (except the fenugreek), oil, & chicken. Simmer, uncovered, on medium heat for 10 minutes.
5. After that time turn the chicken over & simmer, uncovered, for 10 minutes more. (You may use a regular pot if you don't have a pressure cooker. The cook times here are the same).

6. While the chicken is simmering start your second batch of m'semmen, repeating all the steps for it. You should end up with around 25 sheets of m'semmen in all.

7. After the chicken is done simmering add the lentils, smen, fenugreek & another cup of water to the bottom of the pressure cooker. Make sure the chicken is breast side down. Seal with the lid & cook for 10-15 minutes more, after it begins to hiss. It is ready when the chicken & lentils are tender. (If using a regular pot, the cook time is longer, around 30-40 minutes).

8. Take all the m'semmen sheets & shred them into 1-inch pieces. Place them in the top of a couscoussier or steamer. Steam them until they are limp & warm.

9. Scatter a thin layer of shredded m'semmen in the bottom of a large deep platter. Place the chicken in the middle of the platter. Litter the rest of the m'semmen around the chicken.

10. Pour a generous amount of lentils & sauce over the chicken & m'semmen. Put any extra sauce into a bowl with a ladle to be used to dish up additional sauce while eating.

Mrouzia (Moroccan Lamb Confit with Raisins, Almonds and Honey)

Servings: 8

Ingredients:

Meat and marinade:

- 2.2 lbs. trimmed lamb with bones (shanks, neck or shoulder), cut into large pieces
- 2 tablespoons vegetable or olive oil
- 1 ½ tablespoons ras-el-hanout (preferably freshly ground)
- ½ teaspoon ground pepper (a mix of black and white)

For cooking the meat:

- 4 tablespoons olive and vegetable oils (mixed)
- 2 teaspoons ground ginger
- 1 teaspoon smen
- 1 teaspoons salt
- 1 cinnamon stick
- ½ teaspoons saffron threads
- 1 medium-size yellow onion (finely chopped, optional)

For cooking the raisins:

- 1.1 lbs. dark raisins (preferably not too sweet)
- 4 tablespoons clear honey or icing sugar
- 1 teaspoon ras el hanout (preferably freshly ground)

- 1 teaspoon ground cinnamon

Garnishing:

- 5.2 oz whole blanched almonds

Method:

Marinate the meat:

1. First, mix the spices in a large container with 1 to 2 tablespoons of oil. Brush the meat with this mixture and massage it well. Cover and refrigerate 6 to 12 hours.

Cook the meat:

1. In a heavy-bottom pot or a dutch oven, add the meat, the onion, the spices, smen and about ¼ cup of water.
2. Place on medium heat for 10 minutes, stirring a couple of times to rotate the meat, making sure that all sides have been immersed in the liquid at some point. At this stage, we are helping the meat to absorb as much flavor from the spices as possible so these first 10 minutes are important.
3. Slowly add enough water to cover the meat, taking care to pour the water near the sides of the pot and not directly on the meat itself. (You don't want to wash off those spices.)
4. Add the rest of the oil and bring the liquids to a simmer.
5. Continue simmering the meat over medium-low heat for about two hours, or until the meat is tender. During this period, check the pot frequently to see if it needs

more liquid and also to ensure that the meat does not stick to the bottom of the pot and burn.

Cooking the raisins:

1. While the meat is cooking, place the raisins in a bowl and cover with cold water. Leave them to soak for at least an hour before draining and using.
2. Once the meat is tender, add drained raisins, the teaspoon of ras el hanout, and the honey or sugar. Carry on cooking over medium-low heat while watching the process carefully.
3. The sauce should be reduced and thickened after 20 to 30 minutes or so. No watery liquid should remain.

Fry or roast the almonds:

1. The almonds can be prepped for garnish ahead of time or while the meat is cooking. Use one of the methods below.
2. **To Oven-Roast:** Preheat the oven to 325° F (160° C). Spread the blanched almonds on a baking sheet and roast them for about 25 minutes, tossing them a couple of times. They should be roasted evenly throughout with a nice crunch and a golden color at the end. Adjust the time according to your oven in order to achieve the right texture and color.
3. **To Fry:** Pour the oil in a small deep pan and wait until it's warm to start frying the almonds. Oil that is too hot will NOT achieve the desired outcome. Give a stir from time to time and fish all the almonds out once they turn lightly golden. Spread them on paper towels or a kitchen towel to get rid of excess oil.

Serving and storing:

1. Always serve mrouzia hot. The meat is first placed in the center of a warm serving plate, topped with the confit of raisins and followed by any drop of that thick dark amber liquid. The dish is garnished with almonds. Some dried rose petals will nicely finish off the presentation.

2. Keep mrouzia in an airtight container in the fridge for a couple of weeks or in the freezer for months. It's advisable to divide the portions in different containers so It's easy to thaw them as needed. We suggest you keep the almonds separately or fry them as needed. Garnish with them at the last minute.

Notes:

- The recipe makes 8 servings when following the Moroccan tradition of sampling the dish rather than filling up on it. It will serve 4 when offered as a standalone entree.
- When I used to live on my own, I used lamb chops for a faster version which was equally delicious. However, this is a dish that comes at its best after a slow-cooked process.
- It is easier and practical to cook Mrouzia in a dutch oven or a sealed clay pot in the oven, setting the timer and check at regular intervals. This ensures even cooking and reduce the chances of meat sticking or burning. It gives me full control.
- Before the arrival of the modern fridge, Mrouzia was stored in a deep clay urn which was glazed on the interior. A layer of meaty bones would go first,

followed by the raisins and then the thick sauce would be added last. The urn was then covered with an oiled paper and sealed with string. Almonds might also be stored inside but some families waited to add them at serving time.

- It's worth mentioning that the original recipes always had a high quantity of suet added to the sauce which helped with preserving; the layer of oils and fat would protect the meat once the Mrouzia was cooled in jars.
- Traditionally, Mrouzia was shared with all visiting family members and neighbors. The moment somebody showed up at any time of the day, we would heat some and serve it accompanied with bread. As long as Mrouzia was still available, we had to share it. This dish belonged to the community rather than the family who cooked it. At the same time, we were expecting other Mrouzia to come our way. Consider it a family signature dish attesting of the cook's knowledge in making a decent confit.

Mechoui (Moroccan Classic Roast Lamb)

Servings: 4-6

Ingredients:

- 2 kilos leg of lamb at room temperature (or cook longer)
- 100g butter (room temperature)
- 3 garlic cloves (crushed)
- 2 full tablespoons whole (or ground) cumin
- 2 tablespoons whole (or ground) coriander
- 1 or 2 brown onions (chopped in rings)
- 1 teaspoon olive oil + a dash for oven dish
- 1 teaspoon sweet paprika
- salt (to crack freshly before serving)

Method:

1. First, pre-heat oven to 220°C (425°C)
2. Score the lamb's fat (not deeply, only the fat, don't prick the meat or it won't be as juicy).
3. Ground cumin seeds with a mortar and pestle or food processor and keep a few pinches aside for serving.
4. Ground the coriander.
5. Mix ground coriander, ground cumin, paprika, garlic, olive oil and butter to make a paste.
6. Pour a dash of olive oil in an oven dish. Place the leg in it. Move the leg around to spread the oil, you can even massage the leg with oil.
7. Spread the paste with a spoon and massage the whole leg. (You don't have to use your hands if you don't want to, use a spoon or spatula :)

8. Place a few onion rings on top and the rest on the sides.
9. Bake for 10 mins in the oven pre-heated to 220°C (425°C).
10. Baste the lamb.
11. Lower the oven to 180°C (325°F).
12. If you want to use a probe and get the perfect medium/medium rare lamb, let it reach an inside temperature of 51 to 57°C (125 to 135°F). It takes about 12 to 15 mins per 500g at 160°C (325°F).
13. Take it out of the oven. Cover with a sheet of foil and a tea towel. Let it rest for 15 to 20 mins.
14. Slice and serve, sprinkled with cracked salt and freshly ground cumin, accompanied by cooked vegetables, couscous, salad, or any fancy idea.

Notes:

- Use a boneless leg of lamb or one with a bone. Boneless is easier to cut whereas bone adds flavor. I prefer using whole spices that I mix or ground myself with a mortar and pestle or a food processor. The taste is richer. But you can use ground spices.

Moroccan Cow Feet with Chickpeas, Raisins and Wheat

Servings: 4-6

Ingredients:

- 2 calves' feet, cut into pieces (or 8 lamb feet)
- 6 to 8 cloves of garlic (finely chopped)
- 4 teaspoons salt
- 3 teaspoons ground ginger
- 2 teaspoons black pepper
- 2 large onions (chopped)
- 2 or 3 small pieces (2 to 3") of cinnamon stick
- 1 ½ teaspoons paprika
- 1 ½ cups wheat kernels (wheat berries)
- 1 large onion (sliced)
- 1 teaspoon cumin
- 1 teaspoon saffron threads (crumbled)
- 1 teaspoon turmeric
- 1 teaspoon smen (or to taste)
- ¾ cup (125 g) dried chickpeas
- ½ cup olive oil
- ¼ cup golden or dark golden raisins

Method:

1. Soak the dried chickpeas the night before in a generous amount of cold water.
2. When ready to begin cooking preparations, set aside the raisins and wheat kernels to soak in separate bowls of cold water.

88

3. Wash and clean the feet carefully. The hooves can be discarded. In Morocco, the feet will have been charred over coals to remove the fur, but some burnt remnants may need to be scraped off. Also, remove any loose bone fragments. Wash the feet a final time by immersing them in water.

4. Put the feet in a deep pressure cooker or heavy-bottomed pot along with the onions, garlic, spices, smen and oil. Add enough water to come almost to the top of the meat, cover, and bring to a simmer.

5. Cook the meat for 1 ½ hours with medium pressure (or 3 hours if simmering in a conventional pot). Stir and taste for salt, adding more if desired.

6. Drain the chickpeas and add them directly to the pot. Drain the wheat kernels, wrap and tie them in a piece of cheesecloth, and add them to the pot as well. *(Note: If you don't have cheesecloth, the wheat can be added directly to the pot. The advantage of the cheesecloth is that it allows you to create a nicer presentation at serving time.)*

7. Cover and continue cooking with medium-low pressure for another 2 ½ hours (or simmer in a conventional pot for 5 hours – occasionally check on the level of the liquids), until the wheat is tender. You'll need to retrieve the cheesecloth to sample a wheat berry to see if it's cooked to your liking.

8. Drain the raisins and add them to the pot. Cover and continue cooking without pressure to reduce the liquids to a thick sauce.

9. To serve, arrange the meat in the center of a large platter and distribute the sauce, chickpeas, and raisins

all around. Un-tie the cheesecloth and arrange the wheat on top of the meat.

10. Tradition is to gather round and eat communally from the serving platter, using pieces of Moroccan bread for scooping everything up.

Notes:

- The dish can be made in advance. It will keep for several days in the fridge or several months in the freezer. You may want to portion it out when freezing, particularly if not everyone in the family enjoys it.
- The feet and lower leg have relatively little meat, but the tendons, fat and connective tissue around the joints are flavorful thickeners for the sauce, which is where the real appeal of this dish lies. A very long cooking time is required, so the use of a pressure cooker is recommended. Alternatively, the dish may be conventionally simmered all day or overnight.
- Adjust the quantities of wheat berries and chickpeas to your own family's tastes. Moroccans prefer dried chickpeas to canned in dishes such as this, so plan ahead to allow for overnight soaking in cold water. If you do substitute canned chickpeas for the dried, be sure to add them at the very end of cooking so that they heat through without turning mushy.
- The prep time below is for preparation in a pressure cooker; allow substantially more time if cooking in a regular pot. Wrapping the wheat berries in cheesecloth is optional, but it does allow for a nicer presentation of the final dish.

Make-Ahead Vegetarian Moroccan Stew

Servings: 6

Ingredients:

Spice mixture:

- 1 teaspoon ground cinnamon
- 1 teaspoon ground cumin
- 1 teaspoon kosher salt
- ½ teaspoon ground ginger
- ¼ teaspoon ground cloves
- ¼ teaspoon ground nutmeg
- ¼ teaspoon ground turmeric
- 1/8 teaspoon curry powder

Stew vegetables:

- 4 large carrots (chopped)
- 4 (14 ounce) cans organic vegetable broth
- 3 large potatoes (peeled and diced)
- 2 sweet potatoes (peeled and diced)
- 2 cups kale (finely shredded)
- 1 tablespoon butter
- 1 sweet onion (chopped)
- 1 (15 ounce) can garbanzo beans (drained)
- 1 (14.5 ounce) can diced tomatoes (undrained)
- 1 cup dried lentils (rinsed)
- 1 tablespoon honey
- 1 teaspoon ground black pepper to taste
- ½ cup dried apricots (chopped)
- 1 tablespoon cornstarch (optional)
- 1 tablespoon water (optional)

Method:

1. Start by combining cinnamon, cumin, salt, ginger, cloves, nutmeg, turmeric, and curry powder in a large bowl.
2. Melt butter in a large pot over medium heat. Cook the onion in the butter until soft and just beginning to brown, 5 to 10 minutes.
3. Stir in kale and spice mixture; cook until kale begins to wilt and spices are fragrant, about 2 minutes.
4. Pour the vegetable broth into the pot. Stir garbanzo beans, tomatoes, potatoes, sweet potatoes, carrots, lentils, apricots, and honey, into the broth; bring to boil, reduce heat to low, and simmer until vegetables and lentils are cooked and tender, about 30 minutes. Season stew with black pepper.
5. Dissolve cornstarch in water; stir into stew and simmer thickened, about 5 minutes.

Notes:

- If making ahead or freezing, prepare stew through Step 3. Simmer for 5 minutes over low heat; remove from heat and cool in the pot or in freezer-safe container. Transfer to the fridge (store for up to 3 days) or freezer. The vegetables store better if not fully-cooked prior to refrigeration or freezing. When ready to eat, (if frozen) thaw in refrigerator for 24 to 48 hours, then pour stew into a pot, bring just to a boil, and simmer until heated through.

Moroccan Beef Stew with Couscous

Servings: 6

Ingredients:

- 1 package (about 2 lb.) cooked boned beef pot roast with gravy
- 3 cups fat-skimmed chicken broth
- 2 cans (14 ½ oz. each) diced tomatoes
- 2 cups couscous
- 1 ½ teaspoons ground cumin
- 1 ½ teaspoons ground coriander
- 1 onion (¾ lb.), peeled and chopped
- 1 teaspoon salad oil
- ¼ to ½ teaspoon cayenne
- ¼ teaspoon ground dried turmeric
- ¼ cup fresh mint leaves (chopped)

Method:

1. In a 12-inch nonstick frying pan or a 5- to 6-quart pan over medium-high heat, frequently, 4 to 5 minutes.
2. Add cumin, coriander, cayenne, and turmeric and stir until fragrant, about 30 seconds.
3. Add tomatoes and their juice; bring to a boil over high heat, stirring often.
4. Discard any solidified fat from beef and sauce. Scrape sauce from meat into pan.
5. Cut beef into ¾-inch cubes and add to pan. Cover, reduce heat to low, and simmer until meat is hot, 5 to 7 minutes.

6. Meanwhile, in a 2- to 3-quart pan over high heat, bring broth to a boil. Stir in couscous, cover pan, and remove from heat; let stand until broth is absorbed and couscous is tender to bite, about 5 minutes. Pour couscous into a wide bowl.
7. Spoon stew over couscous and sprinkle with mint.

Moroccan Meatloaf

Servings: 6-8

Ingredients:

Meatloaf:

- 2 lbs. ground lamb
- 1 lb. ground beef
- 2 tablespoons extra virgin olive oil
- 2 tablespoons minced garlic (about 6 cloves)
- 2 tablespoons minced fresh ginger (3-inch piece)
- 2 large eggs or 3 medium eggs
- 2 tablespoons fresh mint (chopped)
- 1 ¼ teaspoons kosher salt (or a teaspoon of sea salt)
- 1 yellow onion, finely chopped (about 1 ½ cups)
- 1 large carrot (peeled and finely chopped)
- 1 large celery stalk (finely chopped)
- 1 teaspoon sweet paprika
- 1 teaspoon ground cumin
- 1 cup dried breadcrumbs
- ½ teaspoon ground cinnamon
- ½ teaspoon ground coriander
- ¼ teaspoon cayenne
- ¼ teaspoon freshly ground black pepper
- ¼ cup fresh cilantro (chopped)
- pinch of saffron threads

Pomegranate molasses sauce:

- ½ cup ketchup

- ½ teaspoon of chipotle chili powder (more to taste)
- ¼ cup pomegranate molasses

Method:

1. First, preheat the oven to 350°F. Combine the lamb and beef in a large bowl. Set aside.
2. Heat the olive oil in a large skillet over medium-high heat. Add the onion, carrot, celery, garlic, and ginger and cook for about 5 minutes, or until the onion is translucent.
3. Add the salt, paprika, cumin, cinnamon, ground coriander, cayenne, pepper, and saffron. Cook for 1 to 2 minutes to release the flavors. Remove from heat and let cool for 10-15 minutes.
4. Stir the vegetables into the ground meat. Mix in the breadcrumbs, eggs, cilantro, and mint.
5. Pack meatloaf mixture into a 5x9 or 4x8 loaf pan. If using a 4x8 pan, you'll need to mound the mixture high in the pan. Set the loaf pan in a baking pan. Pour about ½ inch of hot water into the baking pan so it comes up the sides of the loaf pan a bit.
6. Bake the meatloaf for 1 ½ hours, or until firm and cooked through. Let rest for 10 to 15 minutes. Un-mold onto a plate and slice.
7. Serve with pomegranate molasses sauce, ketchup, or just the drippings from the meatloaf itself. Very good served with rice pilaf.
8. **Make the pomegranate molasses sauce (optional):** Mix the ketchup, pomegranate molasses,

and chipotle chili powder in a small bowl. Heat in a microwave or warm in a saucepan until just warm.

Moroccan-Style Brisket with Dried Fruit & Capers

Servings: 8

Ingredients:

- 1 (4- to 6-lb) flat-cut brisket
- 14 dried apricots
- 12 pitted prunes
- 6 medium carrots (peeled and quartered on the diagonal)
- 5 garlic cloves (roughly chopped)
- 5 medium yellow onions (cut into slices ½ in thick)
- 3 tablespoons vegetable oil
- 2 teaspoon packed light brown sugar
- 2 tablespoons tomato paste
- 2 tablespoons capers (drained)
- 2 teaspoons paprika
- 1 ½ tablespoons all-purpose flour (okay to substitute matzo cake meal)
- 1 ½ teaspoons ground cumin
- 1 ¼ teaspoon ground ginger
- 1 heaping tablespoon kosher salt
- 1 teaspoon freshly ground black pepper
- ¾ teaspoon ground coriander
- ¾ teaspoon ground cinnamon
- ¼ teaspoon cayenne pepper
- ¼ cup fresh Italian parsley (chopped)

Method:

1. First, preheat the oven to 350° F and set an oven rack in the middle position.
2. Season the brisket on both sides with the salt and pepper. Lightly dust with the flour, turning to coat both sides evenly.
3. In a heavy flameproof roasting pan or ovenproof enameled cast-iron pot just large enough to hold the brisket, carrots, and dried fruits snugly, heat the oil over medium high heat.
4. Add the brisket to the pan, fatty-side down, and sear until browned, 5 to 7 minutes. Using a pair of tongs and a large fork, flip the brisket over and sear the other side in the same manner.
5. Transfer the brisket to a platter, and then add the onions to the pan. (If the pan seems dry, add a few tablespoons of water.) Cook, stirring occasionally with a wooden spoon and scraping up any browned bits stuck to the bottom of the pan, until the onions are softened and golden brown, 10 to 15 minutes.
6. Add the brown sugar, paprika, cumin, ginger, coriander, cinnamon, and cayenne to the onions and cook, stirring constantly, for 1 minute more. Add 1 cup water and scrape up any browned bits from the bottom of the pan.
7. Remove from the heat and place the brisket, fatty side up, and any accumulated juices from the platter on top of the onions. Spread the tomato paste evenly over the brisket, and then scatter the garlic around it. Cover the pan very tightly with heavy duty aluminum foil or a lid, transfer to the oven, and cook for 1 ½ hours.

8. Carefully transfer the brisket to a cutting board (leave the oven on). Using an electric or very sharp knife, cut the meat across the grain on a diagonal into thin slices (aim for 1/8 to 1/4 in thick).

9. Return the slices to the pot, overlapping them at an angle so that you can see a bit of the top edge of each slice. The end result should resemble the original unsliced brisket leaning slightly backward. Scatter the carrots, apricots, prunes, and capers around the edges of the pot and baste with the sauce; cover tightly with the foil or lid and return to the oven.

10. Lower the heat to 325°F and cook the brisket until it is fork tender, 1 3/4 to 2 1/2 hours. Transfer the brisket to a serving platter, and then sprinkle with parsley. If you're not planning to serve the brisket right away, let it cool to room temperature and then cover and refrigerate until ready to serve.

Notes:

- If the sauce seems greasy, transfer the meat and vegetables to a platter and cover with foil to keep warm. Pour the sauce into a bowl and let sit until the fat rises to the top. Using a small ladle, spoon out the fat. Pour the skimmed gravy back over the meat.

- The brisket can be made up to 3 days ahead of time and refrigerated. Reheat the brisket in a 300°F oven until hot, about 45 minutes. Brisket also freezes well for up to 2 months; just be sure to defrost in the refrigerator 2 days ahead of time.

Chapter Four: Moroccan Dessert Recipes

Halwa Chebakia (Moroccan Sesame Cookies with Honey)

Servings: 6-8

Ingredients:

- 6 ½ cups vegetable oil (for frying)
- 5 cups (4 lbs.) honey
- 4 cups flour (plus additional if necessary)
- 2 tablespoons orange flower water
- 1 ½ teaspoons ground anise
- 1 ½ teaspoons ground cinnamon
- 1 extra-large egg or 2 medium eggs
- 1 soup bowl full of golden unhulled sesame seeds (toasted)
- 1 teaspoon yeast dissolved in ¼ cup warm water
- ½ teaspoon baking powder
- ½ teaspoon salt
- ½ teaspoon saffron threads (crumbled)
- ½ cup golden unhulled sesame seeds, toasted (for decorating)
- ¼ cup butter (melted)
- ¼ cup olive oil
- ¼ cup vinegar
- ¼ cup orange flower water
- 1/8 teaspoon moroccan yellow colorant (or ½ teaspoon turmeric)

- pinch of mastic or gum arabic grains, mixed with ¼ teaspoon of sugar and crushed into a powder

Method:

Toast sesame seeds for the chebakia:

1. Ahead of time, pick through the sesame seeds to remove any debris.
2. Spread them on a baking pan and toast the sesame in a 400 F (200 C) oven for 10 to 15 minutes, or until the sesame seeds are crunchy and nutty-flavored.
3. Allow them to cool thoroughly, and then store in an airtight container until ready to use.

Make the chebakia dough:

1. Grind one bowlful of toasted sesame in a food processor until it turns powdery. Keep grinding until the powder becomes moist enough to press or pack.
2. Mix the ground sesame with the flour and other dry ingredients in a large bowl.
3. Add the remaining ingredients and mix with your hands to form a dough. Add more flour if necessary, to achieve a dough that is rather stiff but pliable.
4. Knead the dough by hand for seven to eight minutes or in a mixer with dough hook for four to five minutes.
5. Divide the dough into four portions, shape each into a smooth mound, and place the dough in a plastic bag to rest for 10 to 15 minutes.

Roll and cut the dough:

1. Take one of the portions of dough, and roll it out to the thickness of a thin piece of cardboard. Lightly flour your work surface if necessary.
2. Use a pastry cutter to cut the dough into rectangles approximately the size of your palm.
3. Make four evenly spaced cuts lengthwise in each rectangle. These cuts should be almost the length of the rectangle, but should not cut through to the edges of the dough. The resulting rectangle will have five strips of attached dough.

Fold the chebakia:

1. Take a rectangle, and thread the middle finger of your right hand through alternating strips of dough. This enables the rectangle to drape over your finger.
2. With your left hand, pinch together the outer corners of dough which hang over the tip of your finger. This will form the center of the flower shape.
3. While holding the pinched corners with your left hand, allow the strips of dough to slide down off your right finger while gently turning them inside-out around the pinched portion.
4. Gently pinch the opposite corners closed once the dough is turned inside out. If done correctly, you'll have formed the dough into an elongated flower shape.
5. Place the folded piece of dough on a baking sheet or tray. Repeat the process with the remaining rectangles and mounds of dough.
6. Gather together the scraps of dough as you work, mold them together into a mound, and return them to the bag to rest before you try rolling them out again.

7. Use up all of your dough in this manner. Cover the trays of folded dough with a towel until ready to fry.

Frying the chebakia:

1. Heat one inch of oil in a large, deep frying pan over medium heat.
2. At the same time, heat the honey almost to boiling in a large pot. When the honey is frothy but not bubbling, add the orange flower water to the honey and turn off the heat.
3. When the oil is hot, cook the chebakia in batches. Adjust the heat as necessary to slowly fry each batch of chebakia to a medium brown color. This should take about 10 minutes if the oil is the correct temperature.
4. If the oil is too hot, the chebakia will color quickly but the insides will not be cooked crispy.

Soaking the chebakia in honey:

1. When the chebakia are cooked to a medium golden brown, use a slotted spoon or strainer to transfer them from the oil directly to the hot honey. Gently push down on the chebakia to submerge them in the honey, and allow them to soak for 5 to 7 minutes. They'll turn a rich, glossy amber color as they absorb the honey. In the meantime, you can begin frying another batch of cookies. *(Note: The longer you soak the chebakia, the more honey they will absorb, and the sweeter and less crispy they become. How long to soak them is a matter of personal preference. However, too short of a soaking will result in pale-colored chebakia that eventually lose their glossy coating.)*

2. When the chebakia have finished soaking, remove them from the honey to a strainer or colander, and allow them to drain for only a few minutes.

3. Gently transfer them while hot to a large platter or tray, and sprinkle the centers with sesame. As you finish soaking other batches of chebakia in the honey, simply drain and add them to the platter in a mound, garnishing each batch with sesame. *(Note: If the honey cools and thickens before you've finished making all the cookies, simply reheat it briefly over medium-low heat. This can be done even if some chebakia are in the pot soaking.)*

Notes:

- Allow the chebakia to cool for several hours before putting them in an airtight container for storage. They'll keep at room temperature for a month or longer, and will freeze well for four or five months.
- Serve chebakia with harira, at iftar for Ramadan, or with tea or coffee.

Lemon Vanilla Almond Ghriba

Yield: 20-24 cookies

Ingredients:

- 4 egg yolks
- 4 tablespoons butter (room temperature)
- 3 tablespoons liquid from preserved lemon (if you don't have this, the zest of 1 lemon will work)
- 2 cups almond flour
- 1 teaspoon baking powder
- 1 teaspoon vanilla extract
- ½ cup granulated sugar
- whole blanched almonds to top cookies
- powdered sugar to coat cookies

Method:

1. First, preheat your oven to 350F.
2. Combine almond flour, granulated sugar, and baking powder in a large bowl.
3. Add to the dry ingredients the preserved lemon juice (or lemon zest), vanilla extract, and egg yolks.
4. Break up the butter with your hands or a pastry cutter and begin working into the dough.
5. Using your hands or pastry cutter mix all of the ingredients until everything has been combined, the dough will feel slightly sticky.
6. From small balls with your hands, about 1" in diameter.
7. Coat the balls with powdered sugar and place onto a cookie sheet or plate.

8. Refrigerate the cookies for 30 minutes, or place in freezer for 10 minutes.
9. Arrange cookies on baking sheet and gently press an almond into the top of each. Do not flatten the cookies, they will naturally shape.
10. Bake for 10 - 12 minutes. The cookies should still be a pale color.
11. Leave on the baking sheet for 5-10 minutes to allow the cookies to finish setting, then transfer to a cooling rack.
12. When the cookies are completely cool, transfer to an air tight container.
13. Cookies can be stored on the counter for 1-2 weeks, or in the freezer for up to 3 months.
14. To serve, remove from the freezer and allow to warm up before serving.

Notes:

- The dough for these cookies MUST be refrigerated or frozen before baking to prevent them from melting.

Fekkas Msseoues (Moroccan Cookies with Almonds and Raisins)

Servings: 30

Ingredients:

- 1.3 lbs. all-purpose flour (plus extra for rolling)
- 5 oz sugar
- 5 fl oz vegetable oil
- 4 ½ oz dried raisins
- 4 ½ oz almonds (skin on washed, drained and pat-dried)
- 3 tablespoons aniseed, roughly crushed (or half aniseed and half fennel seeds)
- 3 medium-large eggs (at room temperature)
- 2 fl oz orange blossom water (or half milk, half orange blossom water)
- 1 teaspoon baking powder
- ½ cup sesame seeds unhulled (slightly toasted)
- pinch of salt

Method:

Ahead of time - prep the ingredients:

1. First, soak the almonds in cold milk or water for at least 20 minutes. Drain and pat dry. Roughly chop them.
2. Wash the raisins and soak them in the orange blossom water for 5 minutes.
3. Sift the baking powder with the flour and set aside.

Make the dough:

1. Mix eggs and sugar in a large bowl with a fork or whisk until foamy. Add all the other ingredients except baking powder and flour. Mix well.
2. Little by little, add the sifted flour with baking powder. If you need any more flour to bring it to a soft smooth dough add 1 tablespoon at a time. Flour absorption differs from one country to another.
3. Work the dough with your hands until a soft dough form. You don't need to knead it.
4. Cut the dough into 4 and roll each one back and forth on a work surface to form a sort of fat sausage or roll of dough about 0.7"/2 cm high to 1"/2.5 cm and 2"/5 cm to 2.5"/ 6.5 cm base. The length of the dough logs will depend on the baking sheet you will be using.

First Baking:

1. Carefully transfer each roll of dough to a baking sheet. Brush the logs with egg
2. With a fork, draw straight lines or crossed lines in the egg-wash but not the dough itself. So, try to have a light hand.
3. Preheat the oven to 338° F (170° C). Bake for about 15 -20 minutes. Since ovens and thickness are different, you should be looking for the following: the rolls need to form a light crust without really being completely baked. We just half-bake them. The texture inside should be a bit soft but already showing a crumbly but compact texture. The outside should be bit springy to the touch.

4. Let the baked logs cool a bit then cover them with a cloth. They need to rest overnight or at least 6 hours. (A faster option is to cover them with a damp cloth for about 1 hour before cutting them.)

Cutting and baking fekkas:

1. With a sharp knife, carefully cut the fekkas into ½ cm thick slices. Cut them slightly diagonal. Be careful not to break them.
2. Place the slices on a baking sheet. If you have added raisins, you need to line your pan with baking paper. As the fekkas will not spread at this stage, you can arrange them touching each other; no need to keep space in between.
3. Bake in a 338° F (170° C) oven until golden brown, about 12-15 minutes. Turn off the oven and leave them inside.
4. Let them cool before removing them very carefully from the baking sheet.

Use the broken fekkas:

1. Serve broken fekkas with milk for a nice morning breakfast. Let them soak for a couple of minutes and eat like cereal.
2. You can also use broken bits of fekkas as a crumble over fruit salads or tarts and over panna cotta or muhallabia.

Notes:

- Respect the resting time between 1st baking and cutting.

- To avoid breakage, it's also advised to chop almonds in tiny crumbs instead of having big pieces.
- The idea of adding instant coffee to the egg-wash is not that old (only about 20 years). It just gives a nice color to fekkas. And just like vinegar, it neutralizes the taste from the yolk. So, if you use the coffee you wouldn't need the vinegar.

Merendina

Serves: 6

Ingredients:

Ganache:

- 200 gr 70% dark chocolate
- 200 gr double cream
- 50 gr icing sugar

Sponge:

- 170 gr caster sugar
- 140 gr plain flour
- 120 ml buttermilk
- 90 ml sunflower oil and more for oiling
- 40 gr corn flour
- 2 large eggs or 3 medium eggs
- 1 teaspoon vanilla extract
- ½ teaspoon baking powder
- ½ teaspoon baking soda
- ¼ teaspoon salt

Syrup:

- 40 gr caster sugar

Coating:

- 300 gr 70% dark chocolate (chopped)
- 40 gr milk chocolate (chopped)
- 3 tablespoons coconut oil

Method:

1. Start with the ganache.
2. In a medium sized saucepan, add in the double cream, chocolate and icing sugar over medium-low heat and leave stirring occasionally until the chocolate is melted and the mixture is well combined, about 5 minutes.
3. Cover with cling film and place in the fridge until the ganache is spreadable, about 1 hour. After 1 hour remove it from the fridge otherwise, the ganache will become very hard and you won't be able to spread it.
4. Preheat the oven to 180C/350F/Gas 4. Oil and line a 39.5 X 27 cm baking sheet with baking paper. Set aside. In a large mixing bowl, mix together the flour, corn flour, baking powder, baking soda and salt. Set aside.
5. In another bowl, add in the eggs and the sugar and use an electric whisk to beat the eggs and the sugar until the mixture becomes thick, fluffy, and triples in size, about 5 minutes. Add the vanilla extract and the vegetable oil, and whisk again for few seconds until the mixture is well combined.
6. Gradually add in the dry ingredients mixture until fully incorporated. Finally, progressively stir in the buttermilk until the mixture is well combined.
7. Pour the batter in the prepared baking sheet and spread the cake mixture evenly all over the pan. Bake for 17 to 20 minutes or until a toothpick inserted in the center comes out clean. Allow to cool completely on a wire rack before assembling.
8. Meanwhile make the syrup. Bring 40 gr of cold water and the caster sugar to a boil over high heat, reduce the

heat to low and stir until all the sugar dissolvers, 3 to 5 minutes. Set aside and leave to cool.

9. Once the cake is completely cool, halve it vertically and brush the surface of the two sponge cakes with syrup. Discard the remaining syrup, if any. Spread the ganache all over one of the sponge cakes and top it with another half. Lightly press the sandwiched cakes to level them and use a sharp knife to divide it into 10 parts to make 10 rectangles.

10. Place the dark chocolate and the coconut oil in a microwave-safe shallow bowl stopping and stirring at 15 seconds intervals until smooth and creamy. Leave the chocolate to cool until it reaches room temperature, about 10 minutes.

11. Use two forks (or a small slotted turner) to dip a sandwich in the dark chocolate, a few seconds on each side to fully coat it in chocolate. Immediately transfer the coated sandwich on baking or silicon paper. Repeat until all the sandwiches are coated with chocolate.

12. Transfer the milk chocolate and a teaspoon of water in a microwave-safe bowl stopping and stirring at 10 seconds intervals until smooth and creamy. Use a fork to splatter the milk chocolate over the coated sandwiches. Leave until the chocolate is firm, about 2 hours at room temperature, 40 minutes in the fridge. Serve immediately.

M'hancha (Moroccan Almond Snake Pastry)

Yield: 1-2 pastries

Ingredients:

For the almond paste:

- 17 oz. (500 g) almonds (blanched and peeled)
- 1 cup (225 g) granulated sugar (or to taste)
- 2 to 3 tablespoons (40 ml) orange flower water
- ¼ teaspoon ground cinnamon (or to taste)
- ¼ cup (60 g) unsalted butter (softened)
- tiny pinch of mastic or gum arabic powder

For assembling the pastry:

- 10 medium-sized (9" to 10" diameter) warqa leaves
- 3 ½ oz. (100 g) unsalted butter (melted)
- 1 egg yolk (slightly beaten, for sealing)
- egg wash from 1 egg beaten with 1 tablespoon water or milk

For garnishing the pastry:

- 1 cup of honey mixed with a little orange flower water
- coarsely ground (or sliced almonds or powdered sugar and ground cinnamon)

Method:

Make the almond paste:

1. First, gather the ingredients.

2. If you are starting with whole, raw almonds, blanch and peel them. Allow them to dry, then fry half of the blanched almonds in shallow vegetable oil until golden brown. Be careful not to burn them. Remove and drain the almonds in a strainer or on paper towels.
3. Place the fried and unfried almonds in a food process along with the sugar. Process until very powdery, then continue processing a bit longer until the mixture begins to turn to a paste.
4. Transfer the ground almonds to a bowl. By hand, work in the cinnamon, gum arabic, butter and orange flower water. Knead until all ingredients are evenly combined into a smooth almond paste.
5. Take a handful of the almond paste and squeeze it into a log shape. Roll the log back and forth on your work surface to make a long stick of paste the thickness of your thumb or index finger.
6. Do not taper the ends. Repeat with the remaining almond paste.

Shape and bake the m'hancha pastry:

1. Gather the ingredients.
2. Preheat your oven to 350 F (180° C). Line a large baking pan with parchment paper.
3. Arrange your round warqa leaves into a neat stack and trim straight across the top and bottom with a sharp knife or scissors to make rectangular-shaped pastry leaves.
4. On a large work surface, arrange three or four rectangles of pastry horizontally, overlapping each rectangle with about two inches (5 cm) of pastry dough.

5. Use egg yolk to seal the overlapped edges of dough. The overall length of the overlapping pastry leaves should accommodate half of your almond paste logs.

6. Brush the connected pastry leaves with melted butter. Line up logs of almond paste along the entire length of the bottom edge of the pastry. Press the logs together into a single long roll.

7. Allow a little empty space of pastry after the last log on the right side; this will allow a small length of hollow pastry to be tucked under the m'hancha once it's shaped.

8. Carefully enclose the almond paste in the warqa pastry by rolling up from the bottom to the top. When the roll is nearly finished, brush the last inch or two exposed pastry dough at the top with egg yolk, then continue rolling to the top edge to seal.

9. Starting from the left end, carefully coil the wrapped almond paste; try to avoid cracking the pastry as you work. The hollow end of the pastry dough should now be at the very edge of the outermost coil. Brush the hollow piece of pastry with egg yolk and tuck it under the coil, pressing to seal it to the bottom.

10. Repeat with the remaining logs of almond paste and pastry dough. You can then add this new length of wrapped almond paste to the existing coil, or shape a second, separate pastry.

11. Transfer the rolled pastry to your prepared baking pan. Brush the top and sides with melted butter then brush with the egg wash. Bake the prepared pastry in the middle of the preheated oven until golden brown, about 30 to 40 minutes. (Note: Some recipes which call for inverting the pastry and returning to the oven to brown the bottom, but it can be tricky to do and it's not

really necessary.) Remove the pan from the oven and garnish as desired.

To garnish with honey and almonds:

1. Heat the honey in a small saucepan until hot and thin. Stir in a small spoonful or two of orange flower water.
2. Brush as much honey syrup as desired over the still-warm pastry and garnish with chopped or sliced almonds. Leave to cool before serving.

To garnish with powdered sugar:

1. Allow the snake pastry to cool, then generously sift powdered sugar over the top.
2. If desired, ground cinnamon may be added to the garnish, either by dusting lightly over the powdered sugar or by arranging thin lines of cinnamon across the top.

Notes:

- *To make m'hancha in advance,* completely shape the pastry, including brushing with the egg wash. Wrap and freeze, then bake the day of serving, allowing extra time if placing the pastry in the oven directly from the freezer.
- *To use phyllo dough instead of warqa,* follow the method described above, but use two or three layers of phyllo for every single layer of warqa, remembering to brush each layer with melted butter. Keep any unused phyllo covered under a damp towel until ready to use it.
- *To shape mini m'hancha,* divide the almond paste into 20 portions. Shape each into a narrow cylinder a little

longer than your middle finger. Cut the round warqa sheets in half, brush each half with butter, then fold each piece in half to make a wedge. Take a folded wedge of pastry and lay it in front of you, wide curve at the bottom. Place a log of almond paste along the bottom (if necessary, roll it back and forth to elongate it to nearly width of your pastry) and roll it up the pastry toward the point, using egg yolk to seal the point to the rolled pastry. Coil the wrapped almond paste and place on the prepared baking pan. Repeat with the remaining almond paste and pastry, then brush all with melted butter and then egg wash. Bake and garnish as directed.

Moroccan Chocolate Mousse

Servings: 4-6

Ingredients:

- 2 cups heavy cream (chilled)
- 1 ½ teaspoons agave nectar
- ¼ teaspoon ground cinnamon
- ¼ teaspoon ground cumin
- 1/8 teaspoon salt
- 8 ounces dark chocolate (70% cacao), chopped

Method:

1. First, stir together the heavy cream, agave, cinnamon, cumin and salt in a large bowl.
2. Place the chopped chocolate in the bowl of a double boiler. Set the bowl over a pot of gently simmering water and stir until the chocolate is fully melted, about 5 minutes. Remove the bowl from the pot and set on a dish towel to dry the bottom of the bowl.
3. Using a hand-held mixer, whip the spiced cream just until it forms soft peaks, 2 to 3 minutes; be careful not to over-whip. Now, using a rubber spatula, quickly and gently fold the melted chocolate into the whipped cream.
4. Serve immediately, or divide the mousse among serving bowls and refrigerate until ready to serve.

Ghoriba Bahla (Moroccan Shortbread Cookies)

Yield: 40 cookies

Ingredients:

- 4 cups flour (approx.)
- 2 to 3 teaspoons vanilla sugar
- 1 ½ teaspoons (7 g) baking powder
- ½ cup unsalted butter (softened)
- ½ cup vegetable oil
- ¼ cup unhulled sesame seeds
- ¼ cup almonds
- 2/3 cup granulated sugar
- pinch of salt

Method:

1. Ahead of time, toast the sesame by spreading the seeds in a single layer and baking in a 400 F (200 C) oven for about 10 minutes; let cool.
2. Blanch and fry the almonds, then grind coarsely.
3. Combine the sugar, butter, and oil in a large bowl.
4. Mix in the sesame seeds, almonds, and vanilla sugar.
5. Mix in about half of the flour and the baking powder. When combined, use your hands to work in enough of the remaining flour to make a dry, crumbly mixture.
6. Use a stand mixer and paddle attachment to mix the dough on the lowest speed for 10 minutes, or knead by hand for 20 minutes, to make a dough that clumps together but is not so moist as to form one uniform mass.

7. If the dough seems to be too moist, add a little flour. Conversely, if the dough remains too dry and crumbly to pack into a ball easily, then add a tablespoon or two of oil. In either case, allow ample mixing time to blend any additions fully throughout the dough.

Shape and bake the cookies:

1. Preheat your oven to 338 F (170 C). If you don't have a special ghoriba mold, line a regular baking sheet with parchment paper. There is no need to grease the ghoriba mold.
2. Take a portion of dough and squeeze it in your hand to compress and mold it. Shape it into a 1 1/2" (3.5 cm) ball, then flatten it in your palm to a smooth disc shape. Correct any cracked edges.
3. Gently press the cookie onto the molded pan or place on your prepared pan. Repeat with the remaining dough. Plan to bake in batches.
4. Place the baking rack to its lowest position and turn on the broiler. Bake the cookies for 5 or 6 minutes, then turn off the broiler and move the cookies to the upper third of the oven. Continue baking for another 15 minutes, or until the cookies are lightly colored with crackled tops.
5. Remove from the oven and allow the cookies to cool a few minutes on the pan. Transfer them to a rack to cool completely before storing in an airtight container with wax paper or plastic between layers.

Notes:

- Instead of using both the broiler and baking method, you can simply bake the cookies at 400 F (200 C) in the upper third of the oven for about 15 to 20 minutes, or until lightly colored with cracked tops.
- How dark to make the cookies is up to you. Traditionally, most shortbread recipes require baking until set and barely colored, but many Moroccans consider pale cookies to be underbaked. These should be baked long enough to achieve a dry crumb at least, but many cooks prefer to continue baking to a golden hue. Take care not to burn them.
- If using the specially molded pan, the dough may be shaped into flatter discs (be sure the edges aren't cracked) with thinner edges to achieve a more dramatic hollowed-out bottom.
- If time allows, bake a few test cookies to see how your dough reacts in your oven. My current oven, for example, heats differently than other ovens I've had, requiring that I bake cakes, cookies, and bread in the upper third of the oven rather in the middle.

Meskouta (Moroccan Yogurt Cake)

Servings: 8

Ingredients:

- 4 teaspoons baking powder
- 3 measures flour
- 3 large eggs or 4 medium eggs
- 2 teaspoons vanilla (or 2 packets vanilla sugar)
- 2 measures sugar
- 1 small container unsweetened, plain yogurt (approx. 110 g or ½ cup)
- 1 measure vegetable oil
- ½ teaspoon salt

Method:

1. First, preheat your oven to 350 F (180 C). Grease and flour a Bundt or small tube pan.
2. If desired, separate the eggs. Beat the egg whites in a large bowl with an electric mixer until stiff. Set aside. (This step is optional; you can add whole eggs in the next step if you prefer.)
3. In another large bowl, beat together by hand or with a mixer the yogurt (reserve the empty container to use as your measure), the vegetable oil, sugar and egg yolks (or whole eggs, if you chose not to separate the eggs).
4. Stir in the vanilla, flour, baking powder and salt; beat briskly by hand or with an electric mixer until smooth.
5. If you separated the eggs, gently fold the beaten egg whites into the cake batter, being careful to incorporate all of the whites evenly.

6. Pour the batter into the prepared cake and bake for 40 to 45 minutes, or until the cake tests done.
7. Allow the cake to cool in the pan for five to 10 minutes before inverting onto a plate. The cake may be served warm, but it will improve in flavor and texture as it sits. Allow it to cool completely before storing in an airtight container.

Moroccan Couscous Cakes

Serves: 4

Ingredients:

- 100g silken firm tofu (cut into 1cm cubes)
- 4 slices wholemeal toast
- 2 large eggs or 3 medium eggs
- 2 tablespoons olive oil
- 1 tablespoon fresh mint (chopped)
- 1 cup couscous
- 1 cup reduced-salt vegetable stock (boiling)
- 1 tablespoon moroccan seasoning
- ½ cup low-fat natural yoghurt
- ¼ cup pistachios (chopped)
- ¼ cup chopped, mixed fresh herbs (such as mint, coriander and parsley)
- large green salad (to serve)

Method:

1. First, place couscous into a bowl. Add stock and Moroccan seasoning. Cover and stand for 5 minutes.
2. Fluff couscous with a fork, then stir in tofu, pistachios, eggs and herbs. Shape mixture into 16 small patties and refrigerate for at least 15 minutes.
3. Combine yoghurt and mint in a bowl. Set aside. Heat oil in a frying pan and cook cakes for 3 minutes each side, until golden.
4. Serve cakes with mint yoghurt, toast and a green salad.

Moroccan Spiced Carrot Cake with Ras El Hanout

Servings: 10

Ingredients:

- 370 g finely grated carrots (about 3 cups)
- 365 g all-purpose flour
- 220 g sugar
- 127 g / ½ cup yogurt
- 127 g / ½ cup apple sauce
- 2 tablespoons almond milk (you may substitute with regular milk or any other plant milk)
- 1 ½ teaspoons sweet ras el hanout recipe in previous post
- 1 ½ teaspoons baking powder
- 1 teaspoon vanilla extract
- ½ teaspoon baking soda
- 1/3 cup unflavored oil
- ¼ teaspoon salt

For the frosting:

- 8oz / 226g one block of cream cheese
- 8 oz / 226g/ 1 cup 2 sticks of unsalted butter
- 7 cups of powdered sugar
- ½ teaspoon vanilla
- ½ teaspoon salt
- the zest from ½ an orange
- ½ cup of unsweetened shredded coconut (optional)

Method:

1. First, preheat the oven to 340 F. Butter and flour two 8-inch-wide and 3-inch-deep cake pans and set aside.
2. Combine the dry ingredients in a clean bowl: flour, Ras El Hanout, baking powder and baking soda.
3. In a separate bowl, whisk together the sugar, yogurt, apple sauce, oil, almond milk, and vanilla extract.
4. Mix together the wet and dry ingredients until it is just combined, be sure to not over mix.
5. Fold in the grated carrots until it is properly distributed in the cake.
6. Divide the cake batter between the two prepped pans.
7. Bake in the pre-heated oven and for 45-50 minutes. The cake should be just mildly springy in the middle once it is completely done.
8. Cool the cake on a cooling rack, and prep the cream cheese frosting
9. To make the cream cheese frosting, simply beat the cream cheese and butter (preferably with an electric mixer), until it is homogeneous.
10. Gradually beat in the powdered sugar on low speed, adding it in one cup at a time.
11. Beat in the vanilla, salt and orange zest. The frosting should be smooth and spreadable.
12. Simply assemble the cake as neatly or as rustic as you wish, and top with the coconut flakes.

Notes:

- Make sure all your ingredients are room temperature, especially the butter and cream cheese for the frosting.

Halwa Dyal Makina (Piped Moroccan Biscuits with Chocolate)

Yield: 120 2-in cookies (120 servings)

Ingredients:

- 3 cups/375 g flour
- 5 ¼ oz/150 g dark chocolate
- 2/3 cup/150 g sugar
- 1 cup/125 g corn flour (corn starch)
- 3 large eggs or 4 medium eggs
- 1 teaspoon vanilla (or zest from 1 lemon)
- ½ cup/118 ml vegetable oil
- pinch of salt

Method:

1. Start by beating the eggs, sugar and oil by hand or with a mixer until thick. Beat in the vanilla (or zest) and salt, and stir in the corn flour until smooth. Mix in enough flour to form a somewhat stiff but pliable dough.
2. Line two large baking trays with parchment paper. Feed the dough through a large fluted tip attached to a manual meat grinder, pastry bag or cookie press.
3. Use scissors to cut the dough into 2-inch strips and arrange the sticks fairly close together on the lined trays.
4. Preheat your oven to 350 F (180 C). Bake the cookies, one pan at a time, for about 15 minutes, or until lightly colored. Carefully transfer the parchment paper with cookies to a rack to cool.

Melt and temper the chocolate:

1. In a bowl, set over a hot water bath, or in a small bowl in the microwave at half power, gently melt about two-thirds of the chocolate. Continue heating the chocolate, stirring frequently, until it's very warm to the touch, about 114 to 116 F (46 to 48 C).

2. Remove from the heat and stir in the remaining chocolate until smooth and cool. Very briefly heat the melted chocolate again, to return it to a temperature of about 88 or 89 F (31 C).

3. Immediately dip the ends of the cookies in the tempered chocolate and place the cookies back onto parchment or waxed paper.

4. When the chocolate has set, transfer the cookies to an airtight container for storage.

Notes:

- The cookies will keep for several days at room temperature, or for up to two months in the freezer. Thaw frozen cookies at room temperature in their unopened container.

Montecaos (Moroccan Cinnamon Cookies)

Yield: 60 cookies

Ingredients:

- 2 cups almond flour
- 2 cups whole wheat pastry flour
- 1 1/3 cup confectioner's sugar
- 1 tablespoon cinnamon
- 1 cup vegetable oil
- ½ teaspoon baking powder
- ¼ teaspoon salt

Method:

1. First, preheat oven at 325F. Line a cookie sheet with parchment paper
2. Combine oil and sugar in a large bowl. Mix well until the sugar has dissolved. Add almond flour, mix well.
3. In a separate bowl, combine flour, salt, baking powder and cinnamon. Add to oil and almond flour mixture. Mix well with a wooden spoon and then with your hands, to form a dough.
4. Using your hands, form small balls. Place them on the cookie sheet and slightly flatten each one.
5. Bake at 325F for 20 minutes. Sprinkle with cinnamon.

Sellou

Serves: 15

Ingredients:

- 2.2 lbs. whole raw almonds (or a little more)
- 2.2 lbs. unhulled sesame seeds (or a little more)
- 2.2 lbs. all-purpose flour
- 1 lb. unsalted butter (approx.)
- 4 tablespoons ground cinnamon (or to taste)
- 2 ¼ cups powdered sugar (or to taste)
- 2 tablespoons ground anise (or to taste)
- ¼ teaspoon salt
- vegetable oil (for frying almonds)
- ¼ teaspoon mastic gum, several drops, ground to a powder (optional)

Method:

Several days or more ahead of time:

1. **Blanch and peel the almonds.** Bring a medium pot of water to a boil. Divide the almonds into several batches. Drop one batch of almonds into the water and return to a boil for 1 or 2 minutes.
2. Drain and immediately begin peeling the hot almonds by pinching the skin off between your fingers, or by rubbing the almonds vigorously in a towel.
3. Repeat until all almonds have been blanched and peeled.
4. Spread the blanched almonds on a towel to dry for several hours or overnight. Be sure they are completely dry before storing in an airtight container.

5. **Clean and toast the unhulled sesame seeds.** If the sesame seeds feel gritty or are visibly dirty, wash them in several changes of water and drain. Spread them out on trays and leave to dry thoroughly for a day or more in a warm, sunny place. Carefully pick through the sesame seeds to remove any debris.

6. Preheat your oven to 400 F (200 C). In batches, spread the sesame seeds into a single layer on a large baking pan and toast for 15 to 20 minutes, stirring occasionally, until the seeds are slightly darker in color, crunchy in texture and nutty in flavor and aroma. (As a stove top alternative, you can toast the sesame in batches in a dry skillet over medium heat, stirring constantly, until nutty and crunchy.)

7. Allow the sesame to cool thoroughly before storing in an airtight container.

8. **Brown and sift the flour.** Preheat your oven to 400 F (200 C). Spread the flour in a very large baking or roasting pan (in batches, if necessary) and place in the oven.

9. Cook for 30 minutes or longer, stirring every 5 minutes, until the flour is evenly colored a light to medium golden brown. Do not burn.

10. When the flour has cooled, sift it several times, discarding any balls that will not break apart or that cannot be pressed through a sieve.

11. Take your time with this step, as a properly-sifted flour is very important to sellou.

12. Store the browned, sifted flour in an airtight container until needed.

13. **Clarify the butter.** Melt the unsalted butter over low heat in a medium or large pot. Continue heating the butter until the milk solids separate to the bottom of the pot and foam forms on top.

14. Carefully skim off and discard all the foam. Place the pot in the refrigerator and leave overnight. In the morning, the butter will have hardened and the milk solids can be poured off. If necessary, rinse the hardened butter and pat dry to be sure no milk remains. This is an important step to ensure that the sellou will remain fresh and unspoiled.

15. Save the clarified butter in the fridge until ready to use.

One day before or same day as making sellou:

1. **Fry the blanched almonds.** Pour ½ inch of vegetable oil into a large, deep-sided frying pan and place over medium heat. When the oil is hot, fry the almonds in batches, stirring constantly, for 5 to 10 minutes, until light to medium golden brown. (If they are coloring faster than this, the oil is too hot and the temperature should be reduced.) Once the almonds are colored, quickly transfer them to a strainer, and then to a plate or tray lined with paper towels. They will continue to darken as they cool.

2. Completely cool the fried almonds before storing or grinding.

Make the sellou:

1. Set up your work area. You'll need a very large bowl or container for mixing the sellou by hand, a fine sieve for

sifting, and a food processor for grinding. Have all ingredients within easy reach.

2. Melt the clarified butter. Set the clarified butter in a pot over very low heat. Leave to slowly melt while you proceed.

3. Sift and blend the dry ingredients. Use a fine sieve to sift the browned flour, 2 cups of powdered sugar, cinnamon, anise, ground mastic gum, and salt into a very large bowl or container. Discard any tiny balls of flour that are trapped in the sieve. Use your hands to toss, stir and evenly combine the dry ingredients.

4. Grind the toasted sesame. Reserve a small bowlful of toasted sesame seeds. Grind the rest of the toasted sesame (in batches, if necessary) in a food processor until nearly a paste. Transfer both the whole and ground sesame to the flour mixture.

5. Grind the fried almonds. Reserve a small bowlful of fried almonds to be stored separately for later use as a garnish. Grind half of the remaining fried almonds to a smooth, moist paste and the other half of the fried almonds to a powdery paste. Add both types of ground almonds to the flour mixture.

6. Blend in the ground sesame and ground almonds. Use your hands to thoroughly blend the ground sesame and ground almonds into the flour mixture. Spend a good 10 minutes or more tossing, blending and rubbing the mixture between your palms to be sure that all is well-mixed and that it's free from balls and clumps.

7. Taste and adjust. Taste the sellou mixture for sweetness and spices. Add more cinnamon, anise or sugar as desired.

8. Add the clarified butter. Slowly and gradually work in the clarified butter, taking care not to add any milky liquid that may have separated in the pot. Mix and knead the sellou with each addition of butter, ultimately using only as much butter as needed to make a glistening, stiff but pliable mixture. (Use less if you prefer a powdery sellou.)

Storing and serving sellou:

1. When all is well-mixed and the texture is to your liking, transfer the sellou to a storage container (or containers). Leave to cool for several hours before covering.
2. Sellou will keep for several months at room temperature (transfer to smaller containers as the volume decreases) or up to a year in the freezer.
3. To serve, loosely heap or shape the sellou on small plates. If desired, garnish with powdered sugar, fried almonds and toasted sesame seeds.
4. Moist sellou can be shaped into petite balls or squares and placed in mini wrappers or liners.

Notes:

- If using mastic gum, the drops can be placed in a small bowl with a little bit of granulated sugar. Use the back of a spoon to crush the drops. (The sugar keeps the gum from sticking to the spoon.)
- It is normal for the oils to rise to the top of the sellou, particularly in warm weather. If this happens, simply stir the oils back into the mixture before serving. If you

feel the oils are excessive, blot them up with a paper towel.

- It is also normal for sellou stored at room temperature to dry out a bit as the sellou continues to absorb the butter.
- Although not as traditional, the almonds may be toasted and ground for a healthier version.
- For extra crunchy texture, coarsely grind a small bowlful of the fried almonds and mix into the sellou.
- Honey may be used in place of powdered sugar. As it adds moisture, less clarified butter is necessary to bind the sellou.
- Instead of clarified butter, some people prefer to use a little oil from frying the almonds.
- Olive oil may also be used instead of butter. It's regarded as healthier but does give a different flavor.

Moroccan Date Bonbons

Yield: 30 bonbons

Ingredients:

- 1-pound moist pitted dates (chopped)
- 4 pitted kalamata or dry-cured Moroccan olives (chopped)
- 2 ½ ounces sliced almonds (½ cup plus 2 tablespoons)
- ¾ cup chopped walnuts (3 ounces)
- ½ cup shelled pistachios (2 ounces)
- ½ tablespoon finely grated fresh ginger
- ½ tablespoon honey
- ½ teaspoon orange zest (finely grated)
- ¼ teaspoon cinnamon
- 1/8 teaspoon ground cardamom
- 1/8 teaspoon orange flower water
- 1/8 teaspoon salt

Method:

1. First, preheat the oven to 350°.
2. Spread the sliced almonds on a baking sheet and toast for about 4 minutes, until golden. Let the almonds cool completely.
3. Grind the pistachios in a food processor to a coarse powder. Transfer the pistachio powder to a plate. Add the toasted almonds to the processor and grind to a coarse powder. Add the walnuts, dates, olives, ginger, honey, orange zest, cinnamon, cardamom, orange flower water and salt and process to a paste.

4. Scoop up scant tablespoons of the date mixture and roll into balls. Roll the balls in the pistachio powder to coat them completely and serve.

Notes:

- The bonbons can be stored in an airtight container for up to 2 weeks.

Moroccan Rice Pudding with Toasted Almonds

Servings: 6

Ingredients:

- 2 ½ cups whole milk
- 2 tablespoons plus 1 teaspoon unsalted butter
- 1 ½ cups water
- ¾ cup confectioners' sugar
- ¾ cup arborio rice
- ½ cup blanched almonds
- ¼ teaspoon salt
- 1 tablespoon orange-flower water (optional)

Method:

1. Start by rinsing the rice in a fine-mesh sieve under cold water until the water runs clear. Transfer the rice to a medium saucepan. Add the water and salt and bring to a boil. Add 2 tablespoons of the butter, cover and cook over low heat until the water is almost completely absorbed, about 15 minutes.
2. Stir in the milk and sugar and bring to a boil over moderate heat. Cook, stirring occasionally, until the rice is tender, about 7 minutes. Stir in the orange-flower water and simmer for 1 minute.
3. Transfer the rice pudding to a bowl and let cool; the pudding will firm up.
4. Meanwhile, in a small skillet, melt the remaining 1 teaspoon of butter. Add the almonds and cook over moderately high heat, stirring, until golden, about 6 minutes.

5. Transfer the almonds to a plate to cool. Sprinkle the almonds over the pudding and serve.

Notes:

- The rice pudding can be refrigerated overnight. Serve chilled or at room temperature.

Moroccan Rifat Cookies

Yield: 40 cookies

Ingredients:

- 280 grams (2 cups) all-purpose flour
- 210 grams (1 ½ cups) whole wheat flour (or spelt flour)
- 150 grams (¾ cup) sugar
- 125 ml (½ cup) vegetable oil
- 60 ml. (¼ cup) water
- 50 grams of sesame seeds
- 10 grams (2 teaspoons) baking powder
- 2 large eggs or 3 medium eggs
- 2 tablespoons fennel seeds
- ½ teaspoon orange blossom water
- zest of one orange
- pinch of salt

Method:

1. First, in a mixer bowl with paddle attachment, mix oil, sugar, eggs, sesame, fennel seeds, water, orange blossom water, orange zest and salt until combined.
2. Add flour, whole wheat flour and baking powder and mix until soft dough is obtained. Knead on for 3-4 minutes until smooth and easy to work with.
3. Cover the bowl with a kitchen towel and let the dough rest for about 1 hour at room temperature.
4. Divide the dough into 2-3 pieces.
5. On a floured surface roll out each part of the dough to a thickness of about 1/2 cm.
6. Using a fork pierce the dough.

7. Straighten the edges with a knife and cut into the desired size cookies.
8. Place on top of a baking pan lined with baking paper.
9. Preheat the oven to 160 Celsius degrees.
10. Bake the cookies for 15-20 minutes or until deep golden brown.
11. Cool completely and keep in a sealed jar for up to two weeks.

Notes:

- If you don't have orange blossom water, use orange juice instead of the water instead. It won't be the same, but will add a delicious aroma to the cookies.
- You can use whole sesame seeds instead of regular sesame seeds.
- Keep the cookies in a jar for up to two weeks.
- The cookies can be prepared from regular flour only (the whole flour is replaced with the same amount of all-purpose flour).

Moroccan Falafel

Yield: 26 balls

Ingredients:

- 400 ml sunflower oil (enough to cover the chickpea balls)
- 150 g chickpeas
- 5 g cilantro
- 5 g parsley
- 3 g mint leaves
- 5 g dukkah spice
- 5 g ground cumin
- 5 g ground coriander seeds
- 1 onion
- 1 garlic
- salt and pepper to taste

Method:

1. Start by rinsing the chickpeas then place them in a large bowl. Add some cold water to the bowl till the chickpeas are more than completely covered. Leave to stand at room temperature overnight.
2. On the next day, rinse and drain the chickpeas, then set aside.
3. Combine chickpeas, herbs (cilantro, mint and parsley), onions, garlic, spices (coriander seeds, dukkah spice and cumin), some salt and black pepper.
4. Transfer to a food processor, and pulse till everything is finely minced. Be sure to scrap the sides and pulse

till all minced, and you are able to squeeze the mixture into a ball that just barely holds together.

5. Transfer the minced mixture to the refrigerator for at least 30 minutes. Then using your fingers, shape the chickpea mixture into small balls of about 1-inch in diameter. The mixture should shape roughly into balls that just barely hold together.

6. Fill a cast iron pan with oil. The oil should be enough to completely cover the chickpea balls. Heat until the oil is very hot but not smoking.

7. Carefully lower chickpea balls into oil one at a time, allowing a little space between each ball. Cook in batches, if necessary. Allow to cook undisturbed until well browned all over. This should take approx. 4 minutes. Transfer cooked chickpea balls to a paper towel–lined plate and season with salt. Repeat with remaining chickpea balls.

Conclusion

Once again, I would like to thank you for purchasing my book.

You now have everything you need to consistently produce traditional Moroccan meals suitable for absolutely any occasion. With dishes for breakfast, lunch, dinner, and desert, you can not only experience every aspect of Moroccan cooking, but also share it with your friends and family.

Just keep in mind that to truly become a good cook you must constantly work towards it. To bring out the flavors of each ingredient, you have to practice, sharpen your skills, and refine your personal taste.

So, take the time to trial every recipe in this book. Slowly and surely you will enter the heart of Moroccan cooking, experiencing some of the best flavors on the planet in the process.

And of course, make sure that you enjoy the process!

Other Books by Grizzly Publishing

"Jamaican Cookbook: Traditional Jamaican Recipes Made Easy"

https://www.amazon.com/dp/B07B68KL8D

"Brazilian Instant Pot Cookbook: Delicious Pressure Cooked Meals Made Fast and Easy"

https://www.amazon.com/dp/B078XBYP89

"Norwegian Cookbook: Traditional Scandinavian Recipes Made Easy"

https://www.amazon.com/dp/B079M2W223

"Casserole Cookbook: Delicious Casserole Recipes From Around The World"

https://www.amazon.com/dp/B07B6GV61Q

CPSIA information can be obtained
at www.ICGtesting.com
Printed in the USA
LVHW081941291021
701790LV00001B/5